PART II.

ZOOLOGY OF THE BOUNDARY.

MAMMALS. . . . . By S. F. Baird.
BIRDS. . . . . By S. F. Baird.
REPTILES. . . . . By S. F. Baird.
FISHES. . . . . By C. Girard, M.D.

WASHINGTON:
1859.

UNITED STATES AND MEXICAN

BOUNDARY SURVEY,

UNDER THE ORDER OF

LIEUT. COL. W. H. EMORY,

MAJOR FIRST CAVALRY, AND UNITED STATES COMMISSIONER.

MAMMALS

OF THE BOUNDARY,

BY

SPENCER F. BAIRD,

ASSISTANT SECRETARY OF THE SMITHSONIAN INSTITUTION.

WITH NOTES BY THE NATURALISTS OF THE SURVEY.

REPORT ON THE MAMMALS.

ORDER

CHEIROPTERA.

Family ISTIOPHORA. Leaf-Nose Bats.

CH.—Molars cuspidate ; nose with a foliaceous or leaf-like appendage, in which the nostrils are situated.

The leaf-nosed bats are easily recognized among the other *Cheiroptera* by the presence of a peculiar appendage to the nose. This, instead of being simple, with two nostrils opening at the end or sides of the muzzle, as in ordinary mammals, is provided with a peculiar appendage of varied form attached to the extremity of the snout, and having the nostrils opening through it. There are four sub-families of the group, which may be characterized as follows:

a. DESMODINA.—Molars presenting a longitudinal sharp edge, and of the minimum number, $(\frac{2-2}{3-3})$. Nasal appendix without any upright leaf; the ears separated ; a triangular bald spot on the end of the lower lip. Anal membrane short or none ; tail wanting.

The species confined to South America.

b. PHYLLOSTOMATA.—Molars cuspidate ; ears separated ; nasal leaf lanceolate, erect, (except in *Brachyphyllum.*) Interfemoral membrane short ; deeply excised ; tail very short.

Of this group one species, *Choeronycteris mexicana*, is found in Mexico. All the others belong to South America. The assignment of a species, *Brachyphyllum cavernarum*, to South Carolina, as well as the West Indies, has not been substantiated by any American author.

c. MEGADERMATA.—Ears large, united ; tragus present.

It is in this group that the species I propose hereafter to describe is found.

d. RHINOLOPHINA.—Ears large, separated ; without a tragus.

The species of this group are confined to the Old World.

MACROTUS, Gray.

Macrotus, GRAY, Voyage of the Sulphur.

GEN. CH.—Nasal appendage with the leaf ovate, lanceolate, erect ; inter-femoral membrane large ; tail long ; free at the tip.

It is to the genus *Macrotus* of the sub-family *Megadermata* that the first leaf-nosed bat ever positively known as an inhabitant of the United States belongs. It is true that the *Brachyphyllum cavernarum* of the *Phyllostomata* has been given as occurring in South Carolina, but the statement has never been verified by any of the large corps of excellent naturalists resident in that State, and is probably an error.

1. MACROTUS CALIFORNICA, Baird.—California Leaf-nosed Bat.

Macrotus californica, BAIRD, Pr. A. N. Sc. 1858.

The ears of this species are very large, scantily haired, ovate and rounded at the tip. Their outer edge extends forward to a little behind and below the eye; the inner anterior edge is partially free; the two ears are connected by a membrane, which takes its rise about one-twentieth of an inch behind the anterior free edge of the ear, and is united to the corresponding strip of membrane of the opposite side, so as to form a kind of roof over the middle of the head, the entrance posterior. The tragus is narrow, lanceolate, naked, one-third the height of the ear. The nasal appendage is short, but rather higher than wide, and extending on the side and beneath the nostrils as a narrow margin. It is coated rather closely with short hairs. The lower jaw is slightly fissured anteriorly, with a small narrow wart on each side the fissure; a groove or furrow extends from the fissure along each side the lower jaw.

The feet are entirely free, the spur about as long; the membrane extending between the spurs is slightly concave, leaving the extremity of the tail free for the last joint, or for about one-sixth its total length.

The general color is a pale brownish grey; darker above than below.

Length to occiput	1.00	Length of tragus	.42
Length to root of tail	2.60	Length of leaf of nose	.30
Length of tail	1.50	Wing from carpal joint	3.00
Length of ears	1.10	Fore arm	2.00

This species closely resembles the *M. waterhousii* of Gray, from the West Indies. It differs, however, in the longer tail and shorter appendage of the nose, as well as in the widely different locality.

2347. Fort Yuma, California. Major G. H. Thomas.

Family GYMNORHINA.

CH.—Nose simple, without a foliaceous appendage embracing the nostrils; teeth cuspidate.

It is in this family that all the North American bats, with the exceptions above referred to, are found, although they do not embrace many different generic forms. The number of species is quite large, though not well ascertained, over thirty being recorded in the books.

In the great uncertainty attending the true characteristics of North American bats, as described, and the necessity of carefully identifying the species of the eastern States, I have been unwilling to attempt the description of the bats of western America at the present time. I have, accordingly, figured but two species; the one, *Macrotus californicus;* the other, *Vespertilio pallidus*, of Major Leconte; the description of which, taken from this eminent author, I subjoin.

2. VESPERTILIO PALLIDUS, Leconte.—Yellow Bat.

Vespertilio pallidus, LECONTE, Pr. A. N. Sc. Ph. VII, Dec. 1835, 437.

"Upper Jaw. Incisors 1—1, large, simple. Canines 1—1, a little concave on the outer side, with an internal, basal, rather blunt cusp. False molars 1—1. Molars first and second, as in all the others; the third with four cusps, three of them transverse, the interior one smaller, and one posterior.

"Lower Jaw. Incisors. 4. False molars 2—2, the anterior one smaller, rather interior. First and second molarsas in others the third with three cusps, not transverse, the interior one larger, and transversely deeply emarginate.

"Hair light fawn colored, tipped with darker, beneath paler. Face hairy, dark brown. Nose rounded, emarginate. Ears longer than the head, oval, entire, very pale dusky brown. Orillon nearly one half the length of the ear, linear, blunt. Membrane thin, naked, brown. Inter-femoral, including the tail, except the two last joints.

"Length, 3; tail, 1.5; naked part, 1; extent, 12.1; head, 9; ears, .95; Orillon, 4."

Inhabits California.

"Differs from all the other species in having but four lower incisors; I hesitate, therefore, to arrange it with the Serinoid or Muroid Bats, and place it at the end of those two families."

Numerous specimens of this species were collected by the Boundary Commission in Texas, New Mexico, Sonora, and California. The one described by Major Leconte was taken at El Paso.

ORDER INSECTIVORA.

3. BLARINA BERLANDIERI, Baird, (p. 53.[1])

Several specimens of this species were contained in the Berlandier collection, and are easily characterized by the above diagnosis. The species is described more at length in the report on the Zoology of the Pacific Railroad Survey.

2159. Matamoras, Mex., Lt. Couch.

4. BLARINA EXILIPES, Baird, (p. 51.)

A single specimen of Shrew, (631,) which I somewhat doubtingly refer to a species described in the report on the Zoology of the Pacific Railroad Survey, as found in Mississippi, was taken at Brownsville, Texas, by Capt. Van Vliet.[2]

631. Brownsville.

ORDER CARNIVORA.

5. FELIS CONCOLOR, Linn. (p. 83.)—American Panther.

1355. Matamoras, Mex., Lt. Couch.—1148. Eagle Pass, Tex., A. Schott.—1005. San Elizario, J. H. Clark.—1110. Copper Mines, N. M., J. H. Clark.

"Panthers are found in greater or less numbers throughout the entire country traversed by the Boundary Commission. In Texas, along all the streams where there are thick bushes, it has been seen from the coast to the Rio Grande, at El Paso del Norte; and likewise from the latter place, in similar localities, was observed by us as far as Los Nogales in Sonora; in which State, the Mexicans, who call it *Leon*, wage against it an unceasing warfare, on account of the ravages which it commits among the cattle. It destroys very many colts and calves in that country, not very often attacking full grown animals. The most effective means used for their destruction, in the hands of the Sonoranians, is strychnine. They poison with this substance the carcases of the animals that have been slain, and not only often succeed in thus killing the *Leones*, but a great number of wolves also.

[1] The page referred to in brackets is that of the General Report on the Mammals of Western North America, forming the eighth volume of the series of Pacific Railroad reports, where the species are described at length, and their synonymy given in detail.

[2] A species of long tailed shrew or true *Sorex*, collected at Fort Bliss, Texas, by Dr. Crawford, was received too late to characterize in this place. A species of *Scalops*, (*S. latimanus*,) is described from Texas, by Dr. Bachman, but it has not fallen under my observation.

"Near Los Nogales, in the month of June, we pursued a female panther, which we succeeded in wounding very severely, the bullet having shattered the hind leg several inches above the ankle. It uttered a kind of howling cry, and fled as rapidly as it could, and disappeared. Six days afterwards we came very suddenly and unexpectedly upon this same animal, lying partly concealed in a fissure among the rocks. Although we were within ten feet of it, when we saw it with its mouth opened, showing its teeth in a very threatening manner, and uttering at the same time a deep growl, it did not offer to spring. As soon as it was killed, we observed the old wound. The weather had been warm and worms were busy in the place where the leg was broken, and the animal had become so emaciated as to lead us to believe that it had remained in that spot during the entire six days, certainly without food, and perhaps without water.

"Those panthers that we have observed were always found in the most solitary places, generally where there were thick bushes, and in the vicinity of rocky spots, affording caverns for secure concealment, and in which to bring forth their young. They always manifested great shyness, and fled rapidly at the sight of us, rendering it difficult to get within gun shot of them.

"On one or two occasions we have heard their cry in the night, when they seemed to be at a distance, but in sight of our camp fires."—(Kennerly.)

"*Felis concolor;* Cuguar or Panther, of the Texans; Leon, of the Mexicans; Chimbica, of the Cochimies of Lower California, Yutin, of the Apaches; Miztli, of the ancient Mexicans; Pagi, of the Chileños; Puma, of the Peruvians.

"A remarkable fact in respect to the panther is related by Clavigero, in his history of Lower California.—(See Book I, chapter 16.) According to this author, the puma exercised so severe a rule over that unhappy peninsula that the work of civilization, commenced by missionary Jesuits, never could rise above a certain elementary state. The missions and presidios established there, after years and years of labor, could never succeed in raising their own supply of domestic animals, but had to depend for that on the States of Sinaloa, Sonora, and other parts of the Mexican empire.

"The prodigious spreading of the 'Puma' over the peninsula of California seems to have been caused by a superstitious belief on the part of the natives there, who did not dare to kill or disturb this animal in any way. It became one of the missionary labors to gradually overcome and remove this singular notion. Indeed, the state of civilization among the California Indians has been so low that they in some respects depended on the success of the sporting puma. Thus Clavigero states that the hungry Indians used to watch the gathering of the buzzards, and searched the ground carefully whenever they observed a number of these scavenger birds, the acute scent of which leads them always unfailingly to the spot where some carcass was deposited upon or under ground By these means these miserable savages were enabled to discover the remains of a puma feast, which such a lordly beast, after the fashion of all the 'Felidae or Canidae' had hidden away here, and slightly covered with soil.

"In the regions of the Rio Bravo del Norte, and other sections along the boundary line, the puma acts a less prominent part. Here he is eagerly hunted by the white and red man, and especially by the cattle-raising sons of the half breed Mexicans.

"The numerous herds of wild cattle, mustang, mules, and horses, besides plentiful other game in the fertile valleys and table lands of the Lower Rio Bravo, Nueces, and other Texan rivers, form a rich support for a vast number of pumas and jaguars.

"The habits of the puma seem to be nocturnal, and it is during the hours after dark that his mournful note is heard resounding through the solitude of the deserts. The note listened to once attentively is apt to make a deep lasting impression

"The different native names as pronounced in Spanish sound very appropriately to the note, and it is likely that the cry of the animal forms the base of its names. The note itself is often several times repeated, with intervals of from two to four minutes. As night time advances, the cry is heard but rarely.

"A puma was killed on the Rio Bravo, between Fort Duncan and Laredo. It was full grown and of considerable size, measuring from the nose to the insertion of the tail nearly four feet. This one was the head of a family, consisting of himself, a mother and two young ones. During his struggle with the hunters and dogs he raised a terrible cry, twice or thrice, to express his rage, and perhaps also to give to his family the notice of danger. The latter seemed to have retreated immediately after hearing the warning, as the hunters, after despatching the old one, could trace the fresh tracks of both the mother and the two young going down on the river side."—(A. Schott.)

FELIS ONZA, Linn. (p. 86.)—Jaguar; American Tiger.

This huge cat replaces on the continent of America the tiger of the Old World, as regards size and strength; little inferior to it in these respects, it is, however, less dreaded by hunters.

The specimens at present before me do not permit any very accurate description of the species, except as to its color. One of these is from the Brazos river, Texas; the other from Brazil. In the former, the ground color of back and sides is of a pale golden yellow, of the belly white. The top and sides of the head, neck, and shoulders, the legs all round, and the belly, are marked with full black blotches, smaller on the top of the head, sides of neck and shoulders; larger on the outside of the legs; largest on the belly and inside of legs. The top of the muzzle is unspotted brownish yellow. Just back of the shoulders on the dorsal line are one or two large blotches, with central light spaces; beyond this, and extending to the tail, is a vertebral series of elongated blotches, more or less confluent, and in contact, and with little or no trace of lighter centres. On each side of this line, the sides of the body are seen to be occupied by several series of large angulated blotches; the exterior black, and more or less interrupted, inclosing an area of the ground color, with from one to four spots of black. No difference of color between the centres of these blotches and the intervals between adjacent ones is discernible, as in the ocelot. There may be traced from three to five series of these blotches on each side of the vertebral line, and they may be made out to occupy the meshes of an irregular reticulation of ground color, and are sometimes alternate, sometimes opposite. The tail is marked with elongated blotches on a yellow ground; towards the tip, however, it assumes the appearance of being black, with transverse light bars. The convexity of the ear is black, with a white blotch.

The Brazilian specimen is much the same with that above described, except that it is considerably larger, and with more red in the ground color.

This species differs in the pattern of coloration from the ocelot, in being without the lines or stripes on the head, upper surface of neck and limbs, these portions being provided with small simple blotches, occasionally elongated. The anterior half of the tail is irregularly blotched, the posterior half only being like the entire tail of the ocelot, black when viewed from above, with transverse light bands. The sets of spots are more regular and distinct, and less elongated than in the ocelot; the intervals between the sets of blotches are of the same color with the centres of the latter, instead of being lighter.

This species is found through the greater part of eastern Texas, extending as far as Red river. It is quite probable that specimens have been killed within the limits of Louisiana, as at present constituted. Southward it ranges through Brazil (where it is abundant) and Paraguay as far south as the Rio Negro.

"This large cat, so common in southwestern Texas, especially along the lower Rio Grande, is rarely seen so far north as El Paso del Norte. The only individual observed by our party west of the latter place was seen in the Sierra Madre, near the Guadaloupe cañon. However, we were assured by many persons of Santa Cruz that it was very common near that village, in the valley of the river of the same name."—(Kennerly.)

Jaguar, tiger, leopard of the Texans; tutinquillé, of the Apaches; tigre, of the Mexicans.

This powerful rival of the puma equals the latter in size and muscular strength and elasticity in the use of its limbs. The habits of both coincide almost entirely, perhaps with the exception that the jaguar confines itself rather to more covered regions, preferring the impenetrable thickets in the river bottoms. Here he lies in wait for his prey, especially on the watering places of mustangs, wild cattle, and deer. Its less extensive geographical distribution, however, gives the jaguar a minor importance when compared with the puma.

As far as my knowledge extends, the head of the Rio Bravo, with the surrounding country, is the northern limit of the jaguar. The westernmost specimen of the genus was seen in the Guadaloupe cañon (Sierra Madre) by Mr. J. Weyss, one of the assistants of this commission.

Many stories about the ferocity of this animal are told among the inhabitants of the western regions, but none substantiating the fact that a jaguar unprovoked will attack man. In the annals of the convent of San Francisco, in Santa Fé, a bloody occurrence is recorded which contains some indications of the jaguar's nature.

The following is an abridged translation from the Spanish:

"On April 10, 1825, a lay brother, after having made confession and concluded his prayers, entered the sacristy. There he was terror-stricken on opening the door and seeing himself almost face to face with a jaguar (tigre) of very extraordinary size.

In a moment the poor man was in the clutches of the beast, which dragged its victim into a back corner to finish the bloody work. The guardian of the convent, on hearing the exclamations in the sacristy, hurried to enter the fatal room, and had scarcely become aware of what had happened when the animal leaped upon his second victim and despatched him with the same promptitude as the first. After a while several other men attempted to enter the bloody sacristy, but not without meeting a similar fate, for the first one opening the door was immediately slain. A senator, Mr. Iriondo, being present, tried now to approach the sacristy by an adjoining back room which communicated with the former by a small door. The jaguar, however, had left the sacristy in the meantime through that very door which Mr. I. wanted to use, and before the latter, followed by a small crowd, could enter it, he heard the cries, "here he is! here he goes! save me!" With this the roaring of the jaguar was heard, and mingled with it the last exclamations of a fourth victim. Each party now retired, the convent people to the church, and the jaguar to where he had chosen his first stronghold.

"Mr. I. now approached and bolted the door of the sacristy opening into the church, making the least noise he could. A hole was then bored through the door, and finally the crowd succeeded in shooting and killing the dreadful monster through the opening thus prepared."

Some explanation is necessary to make more intelligible this almost incredible occurrence. The convent of San Francisco, in Santa Fé, is situated upon the banks of the Rio Bravo, which, after freshets, occasionally overflows the islands in front of the town. During one of these overflows all the animals living in the thickets upon the island seem to have been driven out; among them the above jaguar, which made for the town side, where he entered the gardens of the convent. A low wall only encircles the latter towards the river. From the gardens he entered a small door, accidentally left open, and so came through an old back vestry to the sacristy. At the time his first unfortunate victim entered the sanctuary from the church side the animal was perfectly aware that his retreat was cut off by the river flood, and thus found himself forced to the desperate attack upon a man, which he was likewise compelled to repeat several times.

The largest jaguar skin which I saw was taken from a specimen killed near the mouth of the little stream Las Moras, above Eagle Pass, and measured nearly five feet to the insertion of the tail.

7. FELIS PARDALIS, Linn. (p. 87.)—Ocelot: Tiger Cat.

SP. CH.—Size about that of the American wildcat. Tail not half as long as the body and neck (exclusive of the head.) Ears black, with a white spot. Tail above black, with narrow bands of white; five stripes on the back of neck, with lighter intervals; a dorsal series of full black blotches, sometimes more or less continuous; the rest of back and sides showing a grayish network inclosing angular blotches more or less elongated, black externally, brownish yellow in the centre; those blotches next the dorsal line more serial and smaller.

In size this animal about equals the Texan lynx, weighing rather more than the common *Lynx rufus*. The skull is decidedly longer, its general form not dissimilar to that of the common cat. The fur is short, close, and glossy. The legs are rather long. The ears are large, rounded at the apex, nearly naked around the meatus, around and anterior to which are numerous bristly hairs. The convexity of the ear is covered by a short velvety fur. The whiskers are in four principal horizontal series, the lower ones white, the upper brown. There are naked pads under all the four toes of the four feet, with a larger central one on the under surface of the latter, or five to each foot. On the fore feet there are two additional naked spots above the palmar pad. The tail is nearly cylindrical, tapering slightly to the end, which, however, is blunt; it is covered uniformly all around with hair. In the prepared specimens the tail is less than half the length of head and body together (about two-fifths.)

The general character of the ground color is a dull brownish yellow mixed with dusky; in some specimens there is a more grayish tinge. On this ground is a series of blotches and ocelli of black, sometimes more or less rounded, sometimes much elongated; on the side the spots are included in the meshes of an elongated reticulation of gray; beneath, the color is white, with larger full blotches of black, faint on the lower belly. The legs are spotted all round with full blotches of black, which, on the inside of the fore legs, assume the character of transverse bars. The tail, viewed from above, appears to be black, with six or eight transverse bars of grayish white; these, however, are generally blotches on the upper surface, which sometimes pass around as annuli to the lower surface, and are there interrupted by a narrow break; sometimes they are alternated beneath by other blotches.

The precise pattern of coloration on the body and head is difficult of expression, and varies somewhat with the specimen. The edges of the orbit and the anterior canthus are dusky; the eyelids again and a spot above the anterior canthus are yellowish white. The insertion of the whiskers is shown by four horizontal series of black dots. There is a narrow black stripe, commencing below and parallel with the lower eyelid, and converging posteriorly a little towards another starting from the posterior canthus of the eye. There are several blotches on the side of the neck below the ear, and a row of the same passes across the throat below the occiput, sometimes forming a complete gorget. Starting a little above the eye is a quite distinct black stripe, (those of opposite sides nearly parallel,) and passing to the occiput inside of the ear; between these, on the forehead, are four or five linear series of blotches more or less continuous; the upper part of the muzzle, however, is uniform brownish yellow. The ears are black on their convexity, with a white spot near the posterior margin; the hairs on the concavity of the ear are of a dirty white. On each side of the neck above is a curved black stripe, the convexity downwards; between these are three others nearly straight and parallel, one of them median. They all have the central line (or about one-third) of the light yellowish ground color. On the sides of the neck are a few elongated full blotches, and beneath some few rounded ones in the white ground.

There is a vertebral series of rather angular, elongated full spots of black, which are sometimes continuous for a space, then interrupted. On each side of this may be traced pretty distinctly a series of angular blotches, the centres of the much lighter ground color, and on the sides exterior to these are still larger and more irregularly disposed ocellated blotches, with a greater amount of paler centrally, the black border sometimes not continuous, and occasionally with small full spots of black on the central ground. The intervals between these areolated blotches are lighter and purer than the centres of the blotches themselves; indeed, in one specimen, there is a quite distinct and pretty regular reticulation of grey, with the meshes occupied by the blotches described, namely, an exterior of black enclosing an area of dusky brownish yellow, with an occasional black blotch. On the shoulders are several oblique black lines, and sometimes there are transverse lines of the same on the exterior of the arm.

Measurements.

Point of nose to root of tail, 27 inches; tail to end of vertebrae, 10.50; tail to end of hairs, 11.00; ear above skull, 1.50.

The largest skull I have seen (1358) is 5.30 inches long and 3.46 inches wide.

This species is readily distinguished by its smaller size from the jaguar, the only other spotted cat with long tail inhabiting the United States. There are, however, several species of nearly the same size in South America, to which it approaches more or less. *Felis macrura* or *oceloides*, with somewhat similar markings, is of considerably less size, (not larger than a house cat,) and has a tail as long as the body, (exclusive of the head,) instead of being not half this length. This species occurs in Brazil, where it is very common. The *Felis tigrina* of the Amazon is also a much smaller animal, with about the same length of tail, and the markings resembling more those of the jaguar. *Felis mitis*, so abundant in Southern and Central Brazil, comes much closer to it than any, and is distinguished with some difficulty; it is, however, a smaller animal, lower on the legs, not so much blotched beneath, and the spots on the sides separated by longer intervals and scarcely arranged in series.

Whether or not the present species should bear the restricted name of *Felis pardalis* can only be ascertained from an examination of a large number of South American specimens. Several names of supposed distinct species—as *F. catenata*, Griff.; *F. armillata*, Cuv.; *F. chibiguzu*, *F. griffithii*, Griff., &c.—are usually considered as mere varieties of one.

The skull of the ocelot in general shape is not dissimilar to that of the panther or cougar (*Felis concolor*;) it lacks, however, the depression of the skull at the posterior extremity of the nasal bones, nor are there any traces of the dove-tailed wedges sent up from the parietal bones into the frontal. The post orbital processes are longer, the sides more nearly parallel, and the sides more perpendicular to the major axis of the skull. The upper outlines of the skull are quite similar. The incisive foramina of the ocelot are larger and longer, extending as far as the anterior edge of the canines. The upper canines of the ocelot are more compressed than in the cougar, and have four distinct longitudinal grooves externally. There is but little difference in the shape of the other teeth; the second premolar is perhaps shorter and higher in the cougar. The deciduous dentition is also very similar; the most anterior of the two forward tubercles of the second molar longer perhaps in the ocelot. The coronoid process of the lower jaw is higher, narrower, and with less concave outlines behind in the ocelot. There are also but two distinct foramina on the outside of the jaw below the vacant space separating the canine from molars, and these are in a horizontal line, and sometimes confluent in one, while in the panther there is a third one, equally distinct, above the anterior one of the horizontal series.

29. Eagle Pass, Texas. Col. S. Cooper.—129. Eagle Pass. A. Schott.—255. Matamoras. Lt. Couch.

Tiger cat, Leopard cat of the Texans.—"This beautiful cat, though quite common through the western wilds, was met by our party but once on the lower Rio Bravo. The dogs started it first and 'treed it,' as the hunters say. One or two pistol bullets, however, drove it down again, to seek a safer place in a dense nopal thicket, a common resort of persecuted animals.

"In taking off the skin of this specimen I found its inside all over covered with opuntia prickles, which, naturally barbed as they are, had worked themselves in with the movements of the skin. The animal, however, did not seem to have suffered any, by this otherwise dreaded annoyance, for all the prickles lodged themselves horizontally or in an oblique direction into the skin, so that the points would not reach the muscles and nerves. I observed subsequently the same circumstance on other animals, which accounts for the readiness with which they take to these bushes, unapproachable for men.

"As the ocelot is but a small robber, his importance in regard to the development of civilization stands in a strict proportion to the size of the game he is preying on. He is, however, eagerly hunted for the sake of his beautiful fur.

"Almost every western trapper, of both the white or red race, has something of his professional outfit adorned or made of an ocelot's sk

"One or two dollars are paid for one, and this is also about the price of a Jaguar or Puma skin."—A. Schott.

8. FELIS EYRA, Desm. (p. 88.)—Tiger Cat.

Sp. Ch.—Size of the house cat, but neck longer, and general form more musteline. Tail rather longer than the body, exclusive of the neck and head. Color uniform brownish red, a little paler beneath. (Hairs not mottled?)

The introduction of this species into the fauna of North America is based upon a skull in the Berlandiere collection, together with a short description and figure by Dr. Berlandiere. Although not entirely certain that it is the true *F. eyra*, or that the *F. unicolor* of Traill is the same animal, yet, in the absence of fuller data, it will be safe to consider it for the present as the *eyra*. According to Dr. Berlandiere the animal is "entirely rufous, the head small, ears short, without tufts, body long and slender, tail long. Size of common cat, but longer. Inhabits the desert regions of Tamaulipas, where it is called *onza* and *apache*." He further adds that it is found in the shrubbery along the Rio Grande, near Matamoras, although very rare. The specimen described, to which the skull (1373) probably belongs, was a female, taken very young and kept in captivity a good while without ever becoming entirely tamed.

The figure of Dr. Berlandiere represents the animal as a uniform light reddish brown, without any spots whatever, and no lightening of tints beneath. The ears are rather pointed. The tail is slender and tapering gently to the tip, which is not tufted. The tail is rather longer than the body, by about half the length of the neck. The figure also represents the pupil as vertical; other authors describe the pupil of *F. eyra* as round.

The whole form of the animal is very musteline, as shown both by the skull and the figure. The skull is about as long as that of the common cat (the brain case rather more capacious), but is more elongated and narrower between the zygomata. The neck also is very long.

According to Burmeister the *Felis eyra* is of a clear yellowish red, paler on the belly, the upper lip white, the iris greyish yellow brown, the pupil round. The head and body measure one and a half feet, the head alone three inches, the tail one foot; height anteriorly ten inches, posteriorly one foot. It occurs throughout Guiana, Brazil, and Paraguay, and by the present identification, as far north as the Rio Grande of Texas.

	Felis eyra.	Large *house cat.*
Length of skull (1373)	3.55 inches.	3.55 inches.
Width of skull	2.33 "	2.61 "

The skull of *Felis eyra* is about as long as that of the domestic cat, but considerably narrower and more musteline in appearance. The muzzle is narrower, and the zygoma extends further forwards, so that its anterior extremity falls a little in advance of the second premolar instead of within it, as in the cat and ocelot, and still more in the panther. The free portion of the zygoma anteriorly is narrower than in the cat, and the ante-orbital foramen is double in the specimen instead of single. The flattened portion of the crown is of considerable extent, and reaches to the middle of the nasals, instead, as in the other cats, of involving only the posterior extremities of these nasals. The top of the muzzle is broader, and the sides are much less pinched in and more vertical. Viewed from above the zygomata are nearly straight in lateral outline, the lines converging so as to intersect in front of the incisors at a distance of about two-thirds the length of the skull. The post-orbital process of the frontal and malar (the two almost meeting) are much more anterior in this species than in the house cat. The auditory bullae are more compressed. The occipital foramen, instead of being angular above, is gently curved, the whole representing a regular ellipse, the rather larger diameter transverse. The occipital condyles are larger and more acutely convergent. The occipital outline is less triangular, more pentagonal.

The rami of the lower jaw are narrower than in the house cat; the coronoid process, on the contrary, is higher, broader, and straighter behind.

The outer incisors are larger than in the house cat, the interval between the upper incisors and canines less. The third upper premolar is larger than in the house cat; the central and anterior lobe occupying a rather larger proportion of the tooth; the horizontal section of the tooth is a right angled triangle, the right angle internal, while in the cat it is external. The inner anterior tubercle, so prominent in the house cat, is here almost entirely wanting, resembling the panther more than the ocelot or cat.

The following notice of the present species is taken from Dr. Berlandiere's manuscript:

"This animal, by some called *onza*, by others *apache*, is extremely rare in Mexico, where I have only seen it in the interior States of the east. In the State of Tamaulipas it is found in the shrubbery which grows on the shores of the Rio Grande del Norte. The specimen which I have described is a female, and was given to me when very young. I tamed it, without its losing altogether the habits of its kind, especially when in sight of some prey. It had attained the size of a cat, but was more elongated and slender. In every movement it exhibited great lightness and activity, of which we had many proofs. This digitigrade was in the habit of purring like a cat."

9. FELIS YAGUARUNDI, Desm. (p. 88.)

Sp. Ch.—Larger than the largest common cat; much more elongated in its proportions Tail as long as the body, exclusive of neck and head. Prevailing color a continuous grizzled brownish grey, without any spots. Hairs annulated, and tipped with black. Young rather more rufous.

The existence of this species on the Rio Grande, like the *F. eyra*, is established by a skull (1426) in the collection of Dr. Berlandiere, and a description in his MSS. as *Felis cacomitli*. According to him, "the animal was common in Mexico before the conquest, but is now rare; it is somewhat abundant about Victoria, and a few have been killed on the Rio Grande near Matamoras. Its general tint is greyish, but the hairs, considered singly, are annulated with rufous and black, the tips blackish. It is about the size of the *Felis pardalis*, or ocelot. The female, killed in December, had milk in her teats."

Dr. Berlandiere speaks of this animal as being as large as the ocelot. In judging from the skull, however, it is not much more than half as large, and about one-third larger than the Berlandiere skull of *Felis eyra*. According to Burmeister, the *yaguarundi* is a little larger than the *F. eyra;* of a continuous blackish brown grey; each hair has light ash grey at the base, annulated, and broadly tipped with black. The lips and paws are lighter, the greyish predominating; the whiskers are brown. The iris is brown, but lighter than the fur; the pupil round. Dimensions as *F. eyra*, but the head longer, (3½ inches.)

Skull.—The skull of the *Felis yaguarundi*, in general shape, exhibits a close relationship to that of *F. eyra*, and, like it, much narrower and elongated than in the *Felis concolor* or *pardalis;* calling to mind the mustelas as much as the cats. Like the *eyra*, the top of the head is quite plane and broad; the upper outline curves rapidly from the occiput to above the glenoid cavity; it then slopes downwards almost straight, or slightly concave, to above where the orbital process of the frontal bone begins to spring anteriorly; then making a distinct but very obtuse angle, sometimes in a straight line to the anterior extremity of the nasal processes of the frontal, then makes another angle and slopes rapidly downwards, still in nearly a straight line, to the end of the nasals. The chief peculiarity of the species is seen in the projection forwards of the upper part of the muzzle, so that a line dropped from the extremity of the nasals perpendicular to the plane of the palate would fall very nearly in the centres of the incisors. A similar line in the ocelot, or domestic cat, would fall within the canines. The posterior edge of the intermaxillary, or its suture with the maxillary, is in nearly a straight line, at a right angle, or even more, with the plane of the palate. The sides of the muzzle above, also, are elevated, compressed, and deeply concave, as if squeezed, when soft, between the finger and thumb. The posterior portions of the nasal bones are rather short, and broader than in the ocelot; there is a very decided longitudinal depression in the forehead along the insertion of the nasals between the frontals, as in the cougar. The post-orbital processes are long, and extend perpendicularly outwards and downwards at a more acute angle than in the ocelot. The plane of the zygoma, anteriorly, is more vertical than in the ocelot. The lower jaw is rather short and broad; the coronoid process low and broad, much less attenuated and curved backward than in the ocelot and cat, and broader and less angular than in the *F. eyra*. The skull differs further from that of the *eyra* in the narrower nasal bones, the muzzle projecting more above, and more deeply indented on the sides, and narrower.

The teeth differ from the ocelot, cat, and cougar in the same features as do those of the *F. eyra;* the third upper premolar or sectorial tooth is weaker, and its anterior inner tubercle is nearly obsolete, the tooth sloping rapidly over the fang. The inner angle of the triangle formed by the horizontal section of this tooth is the rectangle instead of the outer, as in the ocelot. Only one groove is visible on the exterior surface of the canines.

Length of skull, (1426,) 3.92 inches; width, 2.49 inches.

This species, according to authors, is found from Paraguay to Mexico, a specimen from the latter country being given by Wagner, as in the Wurzburg Museum. It varies in size, according to different authors, measuring from 22 to 30 inches in the body, (and neck 3,) and from 13 to 24 inches in the tail. The tail is thus about as long as the body, exclusive of the neck.

From the skull, it would appear that the general form, like that of the *F. eyra*, is more musteline than that of the other American cats.

The largest specimens come from Surinam, and it is not impossible that close comparisons may show the existence of two species.

For the introduction of this species, as well as many others, into the fauna of N. America, science is indebted to the liberality and zeal of Lieut. D. N. Couch, of the U. S. army, in purchasing the entire collections of Dr. Berlandiere, and presenting them to the Smithsonian Institution.

"A kind of cat, or at least digitigrade, common in Mexico before the conquest, but at present very rare.

"It is grey, but the hairs considered separately are tinged with rufous and black; their extremities blackish.

"I have been assured that it is killed sometimes in the vicinity of the city of Victoria, the capital of the State of Tamaulipas, and on the plateau of Mexico. On the borders of the Rio Bravo del Norte it is killed in the vicinity of Matamoras. I believe it is not found in Texas."—(Berlandiere.)

10. LYNX RUFUS, Raf. (p. 90.)—American Wild Cat.

This species is abundant in the northern part of Texas, but it is not yet ascertained how far south its range extends.

11. LYNX RUFUS, var. MACULATUS, (p. 93.)—Texas Wild Cat. Called *Gato montis ravin* by the Mexicans.

123. Eagle Pass, Texas. April, 1852. A. Schott.—132. El Paso, Texas. C. Wright.

"*Short-tailed cat of the Texans; gato montes of the Mexicans; no-mē of the Yuma Indians; Chimbi, Cochimies of Lower California.*—In the sierras of Pimoria alta (Sonora) this lynx seems to be quite common, and as we found traces and specimens of it also on the lower Rio Bravo, we may consider its range going from ocean to ocean. The Spanish name of this species points also to its more extended vertical range.

"Our collection contains two specimens, mother and daughter, from the Sonorian mountains, near Fort Yuma, and one individual from the lower Rio Bravo, near Laredo.

"Of the first two specimens, the young one was killed first on the verge of a rock; the instant it fell the mother appeared for its defence, but quickly shared the same fate. The one from the Rio Bravo del Norte appeared one afternoon in front of our camp, on the other side of the river, but on seeing us retired instantly. Our hunters, however, crossed the river, and brought the dogs on the scent. They took the only outlet of a narrow bottom, which was hemmed in all round by vertical banks. Thus the sport was sure, of which the poor victim became soon aware. Besides the barking of the dogs, we heard the valley resound three or four times with the lynx's fighting call. This note, which was furiously thrown forth, was loud and abrupt. It resembled very much, on a smaller scale, the roar of the puma under similar circumstances."—(A. Schott.)

12. CANIS OCCIDENTALIS, var. MEXICANUS (p. 113.)—Lobo Wolf.

This wolf is of quite large size, with a rather narrow head. The ears are large and thickened, rounded at tip, more so than in a skin of *Canis nubilus*, and with a greater amount of hair in the cavity. The feet are large, the pads broad, and of considerable surface. The tail is rather long, exceeding half the length of body and neck without the head; it is covered with long hairs, but is not very bushy, owing to the comparative deficiency of soft fur. The hairs between the shoulders and on the anterior of the back are much longest, and form a kind of mane.

The prevailing colors of this species are a dirty yellowish or dull rusty whitish, with cloudings of pure black, the hairs on the back and upper part of the sides being largely tipped with this color. The lower part of the sides and the under parts generally of the body and tail do not show any black tips in the whitish ground. The throat, however, exhibits a very distinct collar of black caused by dusky tips to the hairs.

The head exhibits a good deal of black shading in the greyish ground. The edges of the lip and the under jaw are dark dusky. There is a decidedly rusty tinge in the ground color of the muzzle, which again reappears as a paler tint in the crown and around the adjacent bases and convex surface of the ears. The band on the throat referred to is five or six inches long, and just in front of the shoulders; it is produced by black tips to the hairs as on the back. The black shading on the sides of the neck is continuous with this, and together they encircle an unmarked space on the upper part of the throat.

The legs are rusty white, deepest on the carpus and on the posterior part of the hind leg. On the fore leg is a narrow dusky longitudinal line of mixed black and greyish hairs, forming a conspicuous mark. There is no evidence in the present condition of the skin of fasciae on the sides of the body.

The tail, like the rest of the body, is greyish white, with the heirs on the upper part and extremity largely tipped with black. There is less of this on the sides, the lower portions of which and the entire under surface are uniform yellowish gray white, except near the tip.

The base of the under fur is rather light brownish plumbeous, varying a little with the region of body; the terminal portion shades into dull yellowish grey, with a tinge of rusty along the back. The long hairs where the black appears are mostly black with a varying central portion greyish white, and sometimes with the extreme base of this color. The black tipped hairs of the tail show this color only on their terminal portion.

$\frac{1050}{193}$. Santa Cruz, Sonora. Dr. Kennerly.

Measurements.

Length from nose to root of tail, (skin much shrunken)	36 inches.	Foot from carpus	$6\frac{1}{4}$ inches.
Tail to end of bone	14 inches.	Hind leg from heel	9 inches.
Tail to end of hairs	18 inches.	Longest hairs on back	$4\frac{1}{2}$—5 inches.
Ears along anterior margin	$3\frac{1}{2}$ inches.	Length of skull	$8\frac{1}{2}$ inches.
Greatest breadth	$2\frac{3}{4}$ inches.	Width of skull	$4\frac{1}{2}$ inches.

In the preceding account will be found the description of what is referable to the *Canis mexicanus* of authors; whether, however, the species is really distinct from that which inhabits the greater portion of North America, I am not able to state. The black chin and dusky collar I have not seen in any other specimens, nor are they mentioned in the descriptions of authors. It will be noticed, however, that the longitudinal stripe on the fore arm, supposed to be a characteristic of the European wolf, is present in this specimen.

The lobo wolf, described in the Berlandiere MSS. as *Canis torquatus*, differs in some respects from this, although agreeing in the main. The skull of Dr. Berlandiere's specimen (1379) is smaller than 2193, but similar in all essential features.

"Near Santa Cruz, in Sonora, we found this animal more common than we had observed it elsewhere on our route. It, as well as the coyote, were often destructive to the flocks around the village. It often, too, attacks the young cattle, both domestic and wild, of this region, which are forced to succumb to its great strength."—(C. B. Kennerly.)

12. CANIS OCCIDENTALIS, var. RUFUS, Aud & Bachm (p. 113.)—Red Texan Wolf.

The red variety of the wolf is said to be very abundant in Texas.

13. CANIS LATRANS, Say (p. 113.)—Prairie Wolf: Coyote.

The question is not yet definitely settled whether the coyotes of Texas and California and the prairie wolves of the Upper Missouri are identical or diverse. The materials collected by the Commission are not sufficiently extensive to throw any decided light on the subject.

128. Eagle Pass, Texas. Sumner, 1852. A. Schott.

Known throughout the length and breadth of New Mexico, Texas, and Northern Mexico as the coyote. During the day it may occasionally be seen sneaking about, but always at a respectful distance; at night, however, there are no bounds to its impudence, not only coming into camp, but stealing your provisions literally from under your nose. It occurs in greatest numbers about settlements; a carcass, however, will not fail to attract a pack in the most barren and unforbidding regions. Camped on a woodless and waterless prairie, the traveller has to wait in some hidden spot near at hand but a few minutes after his companions have taken up the line of march, to have the cheer of living objects in the form of coyotes, creeping in to feed an ever craving appetite upon the offal, or its distant and discordant howl, yet wary of its safe approach. The coat in summer is thin and dirty; in winter, clean and thick. The variety of note and amount of noise a single one is able to produce exceeds belief; their serenades are most usually heard at dusk and in the morning; a fresh scent, however, is liable to excite a howl at any time after night, and no sooner is the key note struck up by a single individual than others chime in from all quarters. The discordant and variable chatter of the cayote has no resemblance whatever to the bark of a dog, and is at once distinguished from the deep, sonorous, melancholy howl of the lobo. The wolf, as a similitude for starvation and poverty, is, perhaps, unequalled, as is indicated by the character of its excrement; this shows that the animal is at some seasons, in some localities, forced to live upon the cactus fruit and grasshoppers, and other matter even more indigestible and more opposite than these, and which must be as little palatable to its natural taste as the thorns that encase its food are disagreeable to its lips.

"Wolves have the bitterest of enemies in dogs; the sharp teeth and rapid snap of the former, however, require but a short time to rid them of the most furious attacks. On one occasion, while at the copper mines, three dogs attacked a single wolf, and, after an encounter of but a few minutes, one returned so lacerated as to cause its death within a week. Notwithstanding this enmity, traces of the wolf are unmistakable, and frequently seen among many of the dogs of Northern Chihuahua and Sonora. The inhabitants here make but two classes of the wolves, coyotes and lobos."—(J. H. Clark.)

"This animal, so common in Texas, is also found in great numbers west of the Rio Grande, extending even to the shores of the Pacific. Generally going in small bands, and frequenting, for the most part, the vicinity of the settlements, they are often a great annoyance on account of their depredations among the sheep and goats, which constitute the principal wealth of many of the inhabitants. And although generally preferring the night for their excursions in search of prey, and preferring to conceal themselves during the day in the grass, bushes, or rocky and solitary places, yet we have known them at El Paso del Norte to exhibit so much boldness as to come within the suburbs of the town, and prowl around among the houses in search of food, while it was yet light, rarely being disturbed by the dogs, with which they even seemed to live on quite familiar terms. Indeed, we have been assured by some of the inhabitants along the Rio Grande, that it is not at all uncommon for the coyote to cohabit with the domestic bitch; but notwithstanding we made great efforts to procure or even see the offspring resulting from this intercourse, we did not succeed in finding one where the proof was indubitable.

"During our march from the Rio Grande to Los Nogales, in Sonora, there was scarcely a night that these animals were not in the vicinity of our camp. Indeed, we have reason to believe that the same individuals often followed us for days from camp to camp, occupying each successive one as soon as left by us, and making a feast of the scattered fragments, and then hurrying on and trailing us to our next stopping place. During the day they were not very often seen, but at night their proximity was generally betrayed by their loud and peculiar bark. This bark is very different from that of the dog, and does not at all resemble the dismal howlings of the large species or Lobo. It is entirely unlike the noise made by any other animal of the prairies, and, when once heard, can never afterwards be mistaken. It is very sharp, quick, and varied, and two or three coyotes, joining in concert, make such a noise as might lead one who had never heard them before to suppose that there were thirty or forty animals present.

"The boldness which they exhibited about the camp when hungry was as surprising as it was often annoying. They sometimes robbed the cooks of what they had set aside for breakfast, even in covered pots or kettles; and should a piece of fresh meat be left hanging on some neighboring bush, it was almost sure to disappear before morning; and sometimes even harness or the equipage of riding animals might be dragged away or seriously injured by them, especially if it had been recently greased, and left carelessly in the night a little distance from the men.

"The coyote is not very swift, and can be readily overtaken on the open plain by a horse of ordinary fleetness; this is a plan sometimes adopted for their capture with the lasso, or shooting them with a pistol.

"I have never known it to attack the larger quadrupeds. It seems to depend mostly for subsistence in the desert regions, and those removed from the settlements, in hunting rabbits, rats, young birds, &c. I have never known it to attack a man, unless wounded, when it defends itself with fierceness and desperation."—(Dr. Kennerly.)

"*Prairie wolf of the Texans; coyoti of the Mexican; coyotl of the ancient Mexican; bay of the Apaches.*—There is no other quadruped forming so prominent a feature in the fauna of our western countries as the coyoti. Its importance in relation to man may be subordinate to that of the puma, jaguar, bear, or some of the ruminantia, but this deficiency is sufficiently counterbalanced by its numeric existence and some usefulness. This animal is called upon on one side to counteract an exuberant growth of organic life, both animal or vegetable, and also to clear the surface of dead matter, which otherwise would infect the atmosphere with unhealthy miasmata. What, too, the coyote may lack in size and muscular strength is sufficiently supplied by its activity, tenacity, and endurance.

"To almost every traveller the coyoti becomes first known by his howling about sunset or sunrise, in which several individuals usually join. This twilight call grows regularly into a piteous whimpering, and is almost invariably preceded by the short and sharp barking of one or two individuals, to which the others fall in instantly. It is, however, kept up only for a few minutes, after which the congregation seem to disperse, each individual following its sport by itself. In the morning about daybreak, often nearer to sunrise, a similar congregation takes place and ends in the same manner.

"To what purpose the coyotis hold their daily meetings can be but conjectured, and may not improperly be put on the same ground with similar gatherings of the crows or migrating birds before their journeys.

"Such gatherings of animals otherwise living and breeding in herds or flocks do not involve particular questions, but with the coyoti, which leads a solitary private life, and joins his kind only before scouting, it is different." —(A. Schott.)

14. VULPES VIRGINIANUS, Rich. (p. 138.)—Grey Fox.

The determination of this animal as an inhabitant of Texas rests on specimens collected on the lower Rio Grande by Mr. Schott. It is found all through the United States, from the Atlantic to the Pacific ocean.

For a full description of the skin and skull of this fox I would refer to the report on the mammals of the Pacific Railroad Survey.

201. Lower Rio Grande, Texas. Skin. Arthur Schott.—130. Eagle Pass? Skin. Arthur Schott.

"The grey fox, or *zorro* as it is called by the Mexicans, is not a very uncommon animal in Texas and New Mexico. In those regions it is generally found along the valleys of the streams where the tall coarse grass or bushes afford it a place of concealment, or in the rocky and solitary places on the hill side. In these spots it will frequently lie still while you may pass within a few yards of it, closely watching your movements, but as soon as it finds that it is discovered it makes a hasty retreat, passing rapidly through the grass or bushes, occasionally making a bound.

"I have never heard it utter any cry whatever, and am much inclined to doubt, as has been said by some, that it either builds its nest in the tops of the trees, among the branches, or even climbs them at all. (See translation of Berlandiere MSS., Art. *V. cinereo argenteus*.) I have seen this animal several times in or near groves of large trees on which the mistletoe grew in great abundance, but never saw in them a nest of any kind that would accommodate a fox, nor did I ever see the animal on a tree or take to one when frightened.

"Although this animal has been found on the Pacific coast in California and Oregon, yet in our route we did not observe it west of the Sierra Madre."—(C. B. Kennerly.)

"*Grey fox; zorro of the Mexican; Colishī of the Apaches.*—According to my observations this animal was more frequently met with in the valley of the Rio Bravo than anywhere else. In the list of the quadrupeds of Lower California a fox is also mentioned, but no description given. Whilst at Fort Yuma I learned from Major G. H. Thomas, then commanding officer there, that two apparently different species of the fox are known in that vicinity. The country forming the head of the California gulf differs so materially from any other in these latitudes that one or two different species of the genus may be expected there.

"The note of the grey fox, which we heard occasionally, resembles somewhat the bark of the coyoti, but is far less abrupt, so that it would be inappropriate to call it bark.

"Though this animal seems to be chiefly nocturnal, it is often met with sporting in broad daylight.

"The rocky clifty banks of the cretaceous formation, together with a more developed vegetation along the middle and lower Rio Bravo, seem especially to favor the haunts of this desert thief more than any other country.

"The natives consider the grey fox a much weaker animal than the common one, as he is easily run down. The specimen of our collection was surprised in a Mexican house at 'Pietras negras,' run down, and killed with a stick.

BASSARIS, Licht.

The species of the genus *Bassaris* look much like a cross between the fox and raccoon, having the cunning look and much of the form of the one, with the ringed tail of the other. The body is more slender than in the foxes, but stouter than in the common weasels; in fact, having much the proportions of the minks, *Putorius vison*. The hair is nearly as long as in the foxes, moderately soft and furry, with longer hairs interspersed. The ears are well developed and erect, pointed and naked on the outer side, but coated on the inner with short hairs. Their posterior edge is split, as in other carnivora. The head is sharp pointed; the naked muzzle quite large; the whiskers very bristly and long. The eyes are rather large. The tail is about as long as the body, quite bushy, though depressed and ringed alternately with black and white. The feet are all five-toed; their under surfaces hairy, except on the pads and balls of the toes, which are naked, and seem to possess a high degree of tactile sensibility. The claws are short and partially retractile.

The number of vertebrae in No. $\frac{1619}{4}$ is as follows: Cervical, 7; dorsal, 13; lumbar, 7; sacral, 3; caudal, 24, with one, perhaps two, lost at the end.

15. BASSARIS ASTUTA, Licht. (p. 147.)—Civet Cat.

SP. CH.—About the size of the house cat. Above brownish yellow, mixed with grey; beneath, whitish. Tail white, with seven or eight brownish black rings.

Size about that of the domestic cat, but rather more slender. Whiskers long, extending back further than the ears. Ears naked externally, except near the margins, where they are scantily haired.

The general color of the upper parts is a dull brownish yellow, with pale hairs interspersed. This tint is, however, much relieved throughout by long black hairs, sometimes imparting quite a dusky hue. The under parts generally are of a yellowish white, with, however, a brownish suffusion along the lower part of the flanks. The tips and edges of the ears, a spot above and below the eye and the upper lip are also yellowish white. The fur is all dull plumbeous at the base and paler at the tip, as described. Of the longer hairs interspersed, some are entirely black throughout, others black only at the tip, the basal portion being paler than the ground color, and producing the effect already referred to. The whiskers are black and white mixed. The basal inner surface of the ears is coated with dusky hair.

The tail may be described as dull white, with seven or eight rings of brownish black and a black tip. These rings are interrupted on the lower side for about one-fourth, so that the central portion of the under surface of the tail is white. The black and white hairs are of uniform tint to their bases, so that one color overlaps the other. These rings become wider and wider from the base to the tip, preserving, however, the same relative proportion of length throughout. Towards the base of the tail the black rings exhibit a considerable mixture of dull yellowish brown, caused by annuli of this color on the hairs near the tip.

A specimen of this species, collected by Captain Marcy, on Red river, in July, 1852, is much purer in its tints, the tail being clear black and white throughout, without any mixture of yellowish brown. The ground color of back and sides exhibits a considerable admixture of greyish ash, especially about the face and shoulders. The black hairs, too, seem concentrated along the middle of the back, forming quite a distinct longitudinal band from the nose to the tail.

Measurements.

	133.		4.			? 97.		
	Inches.	Lines.	Inches.	Lines.	100ths of length.	Inches.	Lines.	100ths of length.
Nose to root of tail	17	6	16	6	....	17	....	....
Tail from root to end of vertebrae	16	....	15	5	....	16	....	....
Tail from root to end of hairs	18	....	17	3	....	18	....	....
Ears, height above notch	1	5½	1	6	....	1	5	....
Ears, width	1	5	1	6	....	1	4	....
Arm, fore foot to end of claws	1	7	1	7	....	1	6	....
Leg, hind foot from heel to end of claws	2	7	....	....	....	....	....	....
Skull, length	....	....	3.20	....	100	3.26	....	100
Skull, width	2.02	....	1.88	....	.59	2.04	....	.63

In the spring of 1852 (April 23) a specimen of *Bassaris* was killed in a hen-roost, near Washington, after it had committed great devastation among the poultry of the neighborhood. It had evidently escaped from confinement, as shown by the marks of a collar around the neck. There was, of course, no indication whence it came originally, but it was supposed to have been brought from California. This specimen is somewhat different from those obtained in Mexico and Texas, although perhaps not specifically distinct. The tail is strikingly different in having the black rings fewer in number and of much greater extent compared with the white portion. Of these black rings there are only five distinctly marked ones besides the tip, and the last or sub-terminal one is more than two inches long instead of about one. Below, the black ring is nearly complete, separated only for the thickness of the vertebrae by the white of the under surface. There is no appreciable difference in the colors of the remaining portions of the body. The ears are decidedly smaller. Very considerable differences are discernible between the skull of this specimen and the others; the cranium is broader, but more constricted behind the orbital processes of the frontal bone; the distance between the zygomata is considerably greater, and the temporal crests of opposite side much closer together. The pterygoid bones, also, are further apart. The proportion of greatest breadth of skull to length is as 63 to 100 instead of 59, as in No. 4, from Texas. Should the examination of further specimens show these distinctions to be such as to indicate a different species, it might be called *Bassaris raptor*.

133. Eagle Pass, Texas. April, 1852. Major W. H. Emory, U. S. A. A. Schott.—4. ♀. Devil's river, Texas. Colonel J. D. Graham, U. S. A. J. H. Clark.

"This cat-squirrel, as it is called by the Texans, lives among rocks or trees; though not a rare animal, its quiet and nocturnal habits renders it inconspicuous, and the procurement of a specimen consequently an unfrequent occurrence. But a single one was seen, and that a female, in the crevice of a rock, with four or five young adhering to the paps. To detach these required considerable force; previous to that time they showed no signs of discomfort, although the mother had been dead several hours. It is said to be a constant and common occupant of Mexican out-houses and deserted ranchos. The specimen obtained, when first seen, was asleep; it fought furiously with claws and teeth in defence of self and home, and displayed no disposition whatever to run off. It is easily tamed and even domesticated, and makes a mild and playful pet."—(J. H. Clark.)

16. PUTORIUS FRENATUS, Aud. & Bach. (p. 173.)—Bridled Weasel.

200. Ringgold Barracks, Texas. J. H. Clark.—239. Matamoras, Mexico. Lieut. Couch.

17. MEPHITIS MESOLEUCA, Licht. (p. 192.)—White-backed Skunk.

This species is said to be quite abundant in western Texas. Its range to the eastward is not yet ascertained, although Berlandiere refers in his MSS. to this or an allied species as occurring at Matamoras.

18. MEPHITIS VARIANS, Gray (p. 193.)—Texas Skunk.

This species is easily distinguished among North American skunks by the great length of its tail, which considerably exceeds the body. The body appears slender, compared with the common *M. mephitica*. The feet are large, the fore claws much longer than the hinder ones (nearly twice.) The palms are entirely naked. The soles are hairy from the heel to the base of the metatarsals, (or for about one-third ;) entirely naked elsewhere. The tail, including the hairs, is much longer than the head and body; its vertebrae about as long as the body without the head.

The hairs on the body are very long and bristly, though lustrous and rather soft. There is comparatively little under fur between the long hair. The hairs on the tail are very long, though shorter at the ends than on the sides.

The general color is a lustrous black; there is a narrow white streak on the top of the head from the snout to the occiput. On the nape, just back of the auditory opening, begins a broad patch of white, truncated anteriorly, and about an inch in diameter; this extends with sides nearly parallel to the shoulders, when it bifurcates and passes gradually round on the sides, and ceases above the thighs. Another narrower line, however, commences in continuation with those just mentioned on each side of the base of the tail, and extends for a considerable distance. The rest of the tail is black externally, but all the hairs are seen to be white for most of their length from the base; there is a white tuft on the middle of the tail, however.

Dimensions.

	No. 127.		No. 233.	
	Inches.	Lines.	Inches.	Lines.
Head and body	15	....	16	1
Tail to end of vertebrae	15	....	$15\frac{1}{2}$	....
Tail to end of hairs	$18\frac{1}{2}$	....	7	....
Longest hairs on sides	$6\frac{1}{2}$	....	....	....
Skull	$2\frac{10}{12}$	....	....	....

This species, in common with *M. mephitica*, belongs to the true *Mephitis*, as restricted by Lichtenstein, and characterized by the presence of four teeth in the upper jaw, behind the canines, instead of three. In both species, however, the soles are entirely naked for their terminal two-thirds. The skull differs from that of *mephitica* in the considerably larger size of the last upper and penultimate lower molar, while the penultimate upper molar is smaller than in *mephitica*. The ramus of the lower jaw has the condyle much more elevated, the distance to the summit of the coronoid process being little more than to the lower angle, while in *mephitica* it is considerably more. The much greater length and amplitude of the tail constitute strong points of difference, as well as the less amount of the basal fur.

The long tailed Texas skunk has, I think, been erroneously referred by Audubon and Bachman to the *M. macroura* of Lichtenstein. This species is characterized, in addition to its long tail, by a simple and continuous non-bifurcating broad dorsal white band, truncated anteriorly, beginning at the nape and extending over the upper part of the tail; thus somewhat like *M. mesoleuca*. There is also a white tuft in the end of the tail. There is, in addition to the dorsal band, a long supplemental white stripe on the side of the body. Lichtenstein expressly remarks on the constancy of the above markings in different skins, while all the Texas specimens I have seen agree with the description I have given, (including two very small kittens from Matamoras,) in lacking the white back and lower lateral stripe.

Mephitis vittata, of the same author, has three white stripes on the nape and one lateral on each flank, with a white tuft in the end of the tail.

The description of *M. varians*,[1] by Gray, is very unsatisfactory; but there can be little doubt that he had this species before him, especially as the locality given is Texas.

This species is abundant throughout Texas, but has not been observed in California. Its southern and northern limits have not been ascertained.

709. ♂. Monterey, Mexico. Lt. D. N. Couch.—237. ○. Matamoras, Mexico. Lt. D. N. Couch.—127. Micr, Texas. April, 1852. A. Schott.—233. Eagle Pass, Texas. Sept. 1, 1853. A. Schott.

19. MEPHITIS BICOLOR, Gray. (p. 197.)—Little Striped Skunk.

Several skulls of a small skunk were collected at Indianola by Mr. Clark, which I refer to this species. No skins were, however, obtained, which throws some uncertainty on the question.

20. TAXIDEA BERLANDIERI, Baird. (p. 205.)—Mexican Badger.

Sp. Ch.—Similar to the *T. labradoria*, but smaller; above reddish gray, with a narrow white stripe extending from the muzzle to the root of the tail.

The differences between skins of American badgers brought from Mexico and those found in the more northern regions of North America have long since been pointed out by Richardson and Bennett, although supposed to be due to local causes entirely, and not indicating different species. I have not had the opportunity of comparing skins from Mexico and the northern United States; but an examination of several skulls in the Berlandiere collection, together with his MSS. description and figures, clearly point out distinctive characteristics. The name assigned by Berlandiere would have been retained, had it not been a so-called barbarous one, and as such not to be perpetuated, if unpublished, however much the propriety of changing it, when properly brought before the scientific world, might be questioned.

Bennett, in referring to this species, says, that with the same general form and pattern the California "variety" has a much darker ground color, of a blackish brown, and grizzled with white on the hinder part of the head. The middle white line shows indistinctly in several places along the back; in fact, the most striking external distinction is seen in the extension of the line on the top of the head, over the whole length of the back to the root of the tail.

Judging from a comparison of skulls, this species is smaller than *T. labradoria*. The true molars are, however, decidedly larger; the outline of the posterior upper one is triangular, the antero-internal angle nearly right angled, its sides about equal. The penultimate molar, too, is broader, with its axis more nearly transverse. In *T. labrodoria* the posterior molar is smaller, the antero-internal angle rather obtuse, and the penultimate molar not so oblique. From these there results a greater interval between these two teeth, which are in contact only externally, instead of being applied against each other for half their contiguous sides. The coronoid process of the lower jaw is less elevated in *T. berlandieri* than in *T. labradoria*, while the condyloid is even higher in proportion.

A younger but quite mature specimen from the Berlandiere collection, with the teeth perfectly

[1] *M. varians*.—Tail elongate; black, with a narrow white streak on the forehead, a large square spot on the nape, and two narrow streaks between the blade bones. Tail black; base of the hairs white. Inhabits Texas.

unworn, although most resembling the others of the same collection, differs in having the true molars still larger. The last upper molar is shaped more like that of *T. labradoria*, but it has three lines of tubercles on the crown nearly parallel with each other. This tooth is of such dimensions that its longest (oblique) axis is equal to the distance between these molars themselves. The skull is narrower and shorter behind; the symphysis of the lower jaw shorter, &c. There is no mark to indicate whether this specimen came from Matamoras; from a widely remote locality there would be little hesitation on the part of any naturalist in making of it a distinct species.

21. PROCYON HERNANDEZII, Wagler. (p. 212.)—Black-footed Raccoon.

1386. Matamoras. Lt. Couch —1052. San Elizario, Texas. December, 1854. Dr. Kennerly.—1053. Devil's river. Dr. Kennerly,

"We found the raccoon quite common at various points on our road as far west as Janos, in the State of Chihuahua, but we did not observe it after leaving the country adjacent to that village.

"It prefers the vicinity of running streams where the bushes are thick, or where there are hollow trees in which it may make its bed. Although eminently nocturnal in its habits it sometimes comes out during the day in the desert places in search of food, especially when it has young. When pursued it takes immediately to the water, swimming with great rapidity and ease.

"We saw them often along the San Pedro river and other streams of Texas in November, along the Rio Grande in December, and very often along the Corralitas river in March and April. When there has offered no opportunity for its immediate escape into the water or impenetrable bushes, we have seen it throw itself back in a state of defence, showing its teeth in a threatening manner, but never heard it utter any cry.

"It is called *Tejon* by the Mexicans of the regions in which we have observed it, and its flesh is highly esteemed by them as an article of food."—(C. B. Kennerly.)

According to Dr. Berlandiere the habits of this species are precisely similar to those of the common raccoon.

Berlandiere speaks of the coati, "*Nasua fusca*," as common in the State of Tamaulipas, one in his possession having been caught in the "Sierra de Tamaulipas del Norte," where it is called apache, sometimes mapach.

22. PROCYON HERNANDEZII, var. MEXICANA, St. Hilaire (p. 215.)—Sonora Raccoon.

Procyon lotor, var. *mexicana*, St. Hilaire, Voyage de la Venus, Zoologie, I, 1855, 25; pl. vi. (Mazatlan.)

A single skin was brought from Espia, Sonora, by the Boundary Commission, which agrees perfectly with the figure and description of St. Hilaire in the Voyage de la Venus, based upon a specimen collected at Mazatlan. These localities are quite in the same zoological province, although somewhat distant. The illustrious author of the mammalian portion of the report of the Venus is quite satisfied that the specimen examined by him differs in nothing from the true *P. lotor* except in the intensity of coloration.

The size of the animal is about that of the average of *P. lotor*. The fur is quite as long as *P. lotor*, and appreciably softer, in this respect differing somewhat from the description of St. Hilaire. The feet appear to be rather slender, and longer than in *P. lotor*. They are scantily haired and naked in patches on some of the phalanges. The tail is about half as long as the head and body, or perhaps longer; it is fully furred with long appressed hairs, and tapers gently from the base to the tip, which is somewhat truncate.

The colors of this animal are similar in pattern to those of the *P. lotor*, but the tints show considerable difference. The body is much lighter and more rusty yellow in its general impression. The long hairs are tipped with dark reddish brown, rather than with black, the reddish becoming rusty on the posterior half of the back and on the sides, the median annulus being a pale rusty white. The under fur generally is of a chestnut brown, tinged with plumbeous towards the base, the colors darkest along the back. The long hairs on the sides generally, as well as on the arm, are whitish to the tips. The feet are whitish above, the hinder ones showing a slight tinge of chestnut on their outer portion.

The tail is tipped with rich purplish chestnut, and exhibits six distinct annulations of the same, with faint traces of a seventh; of these the terminal four only are continued all round, the others being obsolete beneath. The intervals are rusty whitish, and a little larger only than the dark rings. The contrast between the two is not marked very strongly.

The head is marked as in *P. lotor*, the dark patch passing obliquely across the eye is of a dark brownish black; darker than any other portion of the body. It extends back to the line of the commissure, and is there separated from a lighter patch of the same under the chin by a light line prolonged backwards from the edges of the mouth. The sides of the muzzle anterior to the cheek patch and the end of the lower jaw, together with the ears, are dull whitish; the upper and posterior border of the cheek patch is of rather a purer white. The spot behind the ear is plumbeous chestnut brown.

Total length (skin) to root of tail	27, inches.	Fore foot from wrist	3.20 inches.
Tail to end of vertebrae	10 inches.	Hind foot from heel	4 30 inches.
Tail to end of hairs	12 inches.	Length of skull	4.30 inches.
Ear	2 inches.		

This animal, as already remarked, exhibits a close relationship to the common raccoon of the United States, *Procyon lotor*, although, in addition to the shade of coloration, it is readily distinguished from it by the larger and more naked feet and hands, longer, more tapering, and more narrowly annulated tail; the dark annuli being narrower and more distinct. It is in these characters that *P. hernandezii* differs also from *P. lotor*, and it is with *P. hernandezii*, accordingly, that the comparison must be made. There is, in fact, no very appreciable difference, except in shade of color. It is only necessary to replace the black tints on the body of *P. hernandezii* by a dark reddish brown, and the dark brown by a chestnut, in order to reproduce the colors of the Sonora specimen. The chestnut tinge replacing the brown of the hind feet is very slight and quite inconspicuous, except on close examination.

It may be mentioned that the stiffness and coarseness of hair in the Mazatlan specimen, together with the scantily haired condition of the feet, was probably owing to its occurrence within the Tierra Caliente of Mexico. The specimen from Espia, taken in the winter months at a greater altitude, and farther north, is naturally found to be clothed with a much softer and fuller fur.

In some respects this specimen approaches in external appearance the *Procyon cancrivorus* of South America. The latter is, however, much redder in its general colors, the tail longer, with more rings, the cheek patch smaller, being rather a dark border to the eye than a patch on the side of the head. The lower part of the legs is dark brown, and the toes more naked above.

A second specimen was seen by the party of the Boundary Commission, which agreed very well with it in general appearance.

The following table contains the measurements of the skull of this species as compared with those of *P. hernandezii* and *P. lotor*.

Skulls of *Procyon*.	*Procyon hernandezii.* No. 1837. Matamoras.		*Procyon lotor.* No. 898. New .		*Procyon hernandezii*, var. *mexicana.* No. $\frac{2008}{1051}$. Espia, Chihuahua.	
	Inches.	100ths of length.	Inches.	100ths of length.	Inches.	100ths of length.
Total length	4.80	1.00	4.50	1.00	4.40	1.00
From intermaxillaries to condyles	4.67	.97	4.33	.96	4.30	.97
Greatest width	3.17	.66	2.94	.55	....	....
Greatest height above base of occiput	1.50	.31	1.45	.32	1.50	.34
Distance between orbits	1.08	.22	.87	.19	.93	.21
Nasal bones, width before	.60	.12	.55	.12	.43	.09
Narrowest part of muzzle behind incisors	1.08	.22	.97	.21	.96	.21
Upper incisors from front to molars	1.20	.25	1.20	.26	1.13	.25
Upper incisors from front to hinder margin of palate	3.00	.62	2.76	.61	2.60	.59
Upper incisors, width between external edges	.70	.14	.63	.14	.60	.13
Upper molars, length taken together	.93	.19	.80	.17	.90	.20
Upper molars, least distance between	.87	.18	.70	.15	.66	.15
Between line of orbital processes to occiput	3.10	.64	2.87	.63	2.85	.64
Between line of orbital processes to end of nasals	1.60	.33	1.47	.32	1.43	.32
Between line of orbital processes to end of intermaxillary	2.40	.50	2.20	.48	2.20	.50
Orbit to end of intermaxillary	1.67	.34	1.50	.34	1.50	.34

1051. Espia, Sonora. April, 1855. Dr. Kennerly.

23. URSUS HORRIBILIS, var. HORRIAEUS, Baird.—Sonora Grizzly Bear.

Size less than the grizzly of the Pacific coast. Head very broad. Ears and tail nearly equal. Fore claws twice as long as hinder ones. General color dark brownish, with the tips of the hairs much lighter, (of a dirty amber yellow.) No distinct indication of dark stripes on the back and sides.

A single skin of this animal was collected by Dr. Kennerly, at Los Nogales, and brought home. Owing, however, to the excessive heat of the country, the skin appears to have been almost burnt, and contracted to such a degree as completely to obscure the proportions. In its present condition, it is less in size than the average of black bears, while originally the body was nearly as large round, and as long as that of a year old colt.

The prevailing characters of the animal are essentially those of the grizzly of the Pacific coast, in the large feet, elongated claws of the fore foot, &c. The ears are rather short, and completely concealed among the adjacent hair. The tail is very short, and entirely concealed; about as long as the ears.

The feet are very broad and large; the fore claws much larger than the hinder. The longest (removed from the skin) measures four inches along the convexity, half an inch of this, however, is implanted in the skin. The fingers are of nearly equal length, the first and fifth rather shortest, especially the former or thumb; the central claws are longest. The palm is naked, composed of a soft, highly papillose skin. There is a large central pad, rather broader than long, covering most of the foot; behind this, near the exterior edge, is a small circular pad, separated by a deep transverse crease, coated with hair ; the naked balls of the fingers, also, are in nearly a straight line, and separated from the central pad by a transverse furrow, also well coated with hair. On the hind foot there is a single large naked pad, seven inches long, and between five and six inches wide, separated from the balls of the toes by a hairy transverse furrow. These balls diminish progressively from the exterior to the interior; the latter toe shorter than the rest. The longest claw measures about two and a quarter inches.

The hair is coarse in texture generally, and there is little under-fur. It is longest posteriorly and on the sides. The prevailing color of the exterior is a dull pale brownish yellow, with an amber tinge. The tips only are of this color; the basal and larger portion, with the intermediate wool, being of a dark chestnut brown, then passing into a pure blackish nearly to the yellowish tip. Immediately along the centre of the back the blackish tinge in the hair predominates decidedly, as it does (to less extent) posteriorly. The belly and inferior surface of head and throat are nearly of a clear brownish yellow. The legs are of a blackish brown, with a slight tinge of chestnut, the hairs very slightly tipped with yellowish.

There are some points in which this grizzly bear differs from specimens collected on the coast of California, but it will require the examination of a larger number to settle fully the question of permanent characteristics. The ears are shorter, and the tail longer than in the coast grizzly, the two being nearly equal instead of the ears being twice as long as the tail. The central large pad beneath the fore foot is longer in proportion to its width. The fur is decidedly softer, and the colors differently arranged. Thus there is not the conspicuous space along and behind the shoulders, with the hairs uniform yellowish to near the roots, as in the coast grizzly. On the contrary, the hair here is scarcely more largely tipped with yellowish than in the other parts of the body.

Skull. Two skulls of this species indicate very great age in the height of the sagittal and temporal ridges, the obliteration of all the sutures, and the much worn condition of the teeth. Compared with corresponding specimens of the California grizzly, the animals must have been nearly one-fourth less. The profile is much the same as in the California grizzly; in the oldest specimen (990) curving rapidly up from the occiput over the posterior third of the parietal bones, thus passing in a straight but slightly ascending line as far as over the posterior third of the frontal, then sloping rapidly downwards to the end of the nose, at first in almost a straight line, then gently concave. In one specimen the broad forehead is slightly concave transversely, in another it is straight; the orbital process in each being very convex externally. There is, however, no convexity in either specimen between these processes in either a longitudinal or transverse direction.

The point of greatest elevation of the profile curve marks the place where the sagittal crest bifurcates, and is continued on each side as a distinct temporal ridge, elevated above the plane of the forehead.

The under surface of the head is decidedly hollowed out, the lower profile exhibiting a considerable concavity, in this respect approaching the Polar bear. Thus a straight line tangent to the bottom of the notch between the occipital condyles and to the end of the intermaxillary will pass three-quarters of an inch above the palate.

A careful comparison of specimens of the grizzly bear, collected by the Commission, with a series from the Pacific coast, exhibits certain differences, which seem to be of importance. In the first place, as already remarked, the size of the animal is considerably less, probably by about one-fourth. The skull is also broader. Thus comparing No. 995 from the Coppermines, which is very young, but has all its permanent teeth, with 1220 from Monterey, in which all the teeth are in place, except the canines, which are about half way out, we find the former to be a very little longer, but with the zygomata .55 apart instead of .52. This difference lies in the size of the temporal fossae, the cranium proper being largest in 1220. The orbital processes are situated farther forward; the zygoma is longer, especially when measured on its free lower margin. The profile is much the same. The muzzle is narrower and more slender. Viewed laterally, the muzzle is seen to be lower than in the California grizzly, especially above the malar bone. The malar is much lower anteriorly, and the portion extending towards the anterior canthus is shorter and narrower. The distance from incisors to end of molars, as well as to end of palate, is half an inch less, though the animal is older, and the skull a little longer. The palate is more vaulted.

The lower jaw of No. 995 differs from the California specimen in being lower and having the coronoid process longer along its base. The distance from the back of the condyle to the first molar is about one-third the distance to the end of the incissors, instead of one-fourth, as in No. 1220.

The differences in the teeth of the two specimens are quite appreciable. As a general thing those of 995 are in every way much smaller in all dimensions than in the other, though considerably larger than in *U. americanus*. The three posterior upper molars measure 2.62 inches in the one, in the other 3 inches. The chief disproportion is in the posterior molar. This molar has the usual three tubercles or lobes along the inner edge and the two outer ones; instead of having the posterior half of the tooth behind the second outer and exterior to the second and third inner tubercles, sloping obliquely outwards and upwards, and with a general wrinkling of the enamel only, there is a third outer tubercle midway between the middle one and the posterior extremity of the tooth. The narrow space between this tubercle (which is not so high as those anterior to it) is occupied by a few enamel granules. The space between the two marginal series of tubercles is much less. The third upper molar from the end is broader. As in other species the crown of this tooth is divided longitudinally by a deep ravine, exterior to which is a series of two-pointed and trenchant tubercles, the posterior one of which exhibits a supplementary notch behind. The inner side of this ravine is occupied by a series of low tubercles, separated by furrows, both on the summit and inner side of the tooth; the central tubercle rather longest. In the other skull there is but a single trenchant or compressed tubercle, without any trace of subdivision.

The lower molars are very similar in the two specimens, except that they are smaller and narrower in No. 995. In both the posterior molar is triangular, the base anterior; in No. 995, however, the width is about three-fourths the length, and the whole tooth is considerably shorter than the second in advance of it, instead of being nearly equal, as in the Pacific specimen, where, also, the width of the tooth is little more than half the length.

The comparison of large skulls brought in by the Boundary Commission with corresponding ones from the California coast exhibits much the same differences as to the teeth; the bi-lobed or tri-lobed character of the inner half of the first large upper molar being maintained, as also the proportional inferiority in the size of the teeth, and the short longitudinal dimensions of the posterior molar above. The posterior root of the zygomatic arch, viewed from above, is narrower and more emarginated behind and before. The base of the head is much more arched longitudinally, in this respect approaching the Polar bear It has been already stated that a straight line tangent to the occiput and intermaxillary passes three-quarters of an inch from the bottom of the palate, instead of less than half an inch, as in the California bears.

As the result of the above comparisons, I have come to the conclusion that the grizzly bear of the southern Rocky mountains differs appreciably from the grizzly of the Pacific coast in smaller size, smaller teeth, rather broader head, and the other features adduced above, so that there is no difficulty in distinguishing them. Whether this is indicative of a different species or merely of a local race, I cannot say; an examination of corresponding specimens from the Upper Missouri, which I hope hereafter to make, will throw much light on the subject.

I have had no means of comparing the adult skulls of this bear with those of *U. arctos* of Europe. The latter species, however, as shown by a two year old skull, 1033, from Sweden, is considerably broader. The teeth are of much the same size, those of *arctos* rather larger. The last upper molar in the European bear has the posterior half more free from tubercles and more twisted, and the wrinkles on the crowns are finer and more numerous. The third molar from behind is much narrower in *U. arctos*, in this respect even exceeding the California grizzly; the inner lobe is single and much reduced in size. The posterior lower molars are of smaller shape and proportion.

This bear exceeds the *Ursus americanus* and *cinnamoneus* very much in size, and has other differences, which are readily appreciable. The arch of the head does not extend in a uniform convex curve, as in these species, and the forehead is plane and even concave; the anterior portion of the dorsal outline is usually convex in the small species. The proportional width of the head is less in the present species; the muzzle is longer. The zygomatic arch is more massive, especially the posterior portion, which is as high or higher than the anterior, instead of being considerably less. There is a much greater concavity of the posterior half of the palate than in *Ursus americanus,* where this is quite convex, and with various ridges not seen in the present species. The notch of the palate is distant from the posterior upper molar by the length of the latter tooth, while this distance is considerably greater in the smaller bears.

The most appreciable differences, however, next to the shape of the zygoma, size and proportion of the head, &c., are found in the teeth. These are proportionably very much larger than in *U. cinnamoneus,* and appreciably exceed those of *U. americanus.* The third upper molar from behind is, in particular, larger, broader, and with two or three lobes on the inner half, instead of a single and much smaller one. The crowns of the molars generally are more tuberculated, and less finely wrinkled than in *U. americanus.*

Skull.	990 ♂ Copper mines. Inches.	990 ♂ Copper mines. 100th of length.	Skull.	990 ♂ Copper mines. Inches.	990 ♂ Copper mines. 100th of length.
Total length	14.20	1.00	Upper incisors, width between external edges	1.87	.13
From end of intermaxillary to end of condyles	13.10	.92	Upper molars, length taken together	2.80	.19
Greatest width	8.20	.58	Upper molars, least distance between	1.80	.12
Greatest height above base of cranium	4.40	.30	From intermaxillary to commencement of orbit	5.70	.40
Distance between orbits	3.10	.21	Between post-orbital points of occiput	7.80	.54
Distance between orbital processes	4.70	.33	From post-orbital points to end of nasals	4.64	.32
Nasal bones, width before	1.40	.09	From post-orbital points to end of intermaxillary	7.40	.53
Narrowest part of muzzle behind canines	2.80	.19			
Upper incisors from front to molars	3.20	.22			
Upper incisors to hinder margin of palate	6.95	.48			

147. ♂. Los Nogales, Sonora, June, 1855. Dr. Kennerly.—990—995. ♂. Copper mines, N. Mex. J. H. Clark; skull.

"The black bear is the most common in southwestern Texas. A brown bear occurs here also, which I think can be hardly identical with the brown or grizzly of northern Chihuahua and Sonora. The brown bear of the former place is smaller, and is most usually met about water courses; these furnishing both cover and food, it is true there is but little inducement for it to wander out on the open prairie. The black or grizzly was found abundant in all the mountainous regions traversed west of Rio Grande. Late in the summer they leave the mountains for the open prairie, it is said by frontiersmen, for some plant which is relished much, and which ripens at this season. What that plant is I was never able to ascertain. As far as my observation extended, they make an annual migration from the rugged and unfrequented mountain, which they habitually inhabit late in summer, and probably because the supply of acorns, piñones, and cedar berries, their principal food, is exhausted at this season. Its habitat in the mountains is marked by upturned rocks, which seemed to be displaced for the sake of insects and other animals harboring under them, and loose soil torn up in pursuit of the roots of the cedar and other trees. Notwithstanding its awkward and ungainly gait, where the country is at all rough and broken, it will easily outdistance a mule. I have known this bear, when surprised and suddenly startled, to make a snuffling blow, or a respiratory grunt, which is, I believe, the only sound it is capable of producing. Once entering a grassy depression of prairie near the Cobre, I was surprised to see three of these bears sitting on their haunches at a short distance, to all appearances, calmly watching our approach; it was soon evident that they were only reconnoitering, for no sooner did they get the scent of us, than they put off at as rapid a rate as possible. As a rule, they avoid the vicinity of man; yet they have been known to come into camp after the offal after night, and even in day."—(J. H. Clark.)

"In regard to the bears that are found along the northern frontier of Mexico and the southern portion of New Mexico, there seems to be some confusion. In addition to the common black bear, *Ursus americanus*, and the large grizzly, *U. ferox*, there is found another animal, intermediate in size to these, generally of a brownish color, with the tips of the hairs often silvered, especially in the old individuals, and in appearance, except size, is almost identical with the *U. ferox* found in such great numbers n California. Among the people of the country they are known as *brown bears;* but this term is variously modified by the most experienced hunters, as we have heard applied by them, to the same individual, the names grizzly bear, touch of the grizzly, cross between grizzly and brown bear, and common brown bear; but on no occasion have we heard them assign any relationship between these animals and the common black bear, causing us to believe that there must be a considerable difference between this animal and the brown bear of Oregon, which is called by naturalists only a variety of the black; in fact, its size, generally, would necessarily preclude such comparison, while even the very old individual falls far short of the weight and dimensions of the *U. ferox* of California, of which we could much more easily consider it a variety than of the *U. americanus.*

"These animals were observed by us in greater or less numbers in the San Luis mountains, the Sierra Madre, and at Los Nogales; being particularly numerous at the first and last named localities. We were assured by the Mexicans of Sonora, who also distinguished this animal from the grizzly, that it was feared by themselves, as well as by the Indians, more than the latter, on account of its ferocity. This, however, admits of a considerable degree of doubt; for, notwithstanding some very good proofs of its boldness within our own knowledge, we also observed almost unexampled evidence of its cowardice. While, on one occasion, a very old male rushed unexpectedly from the bushes and made a fierce and unprovoked attack upon a gentleman of the Boundary Commission, who, probably, only saved his life by a fortunate escape into a neighboring tree, we observed, on a subsequent occasion, in the same vicinity, a female entirely forsake her cubs by a rapid retreat, and without being wounded; an this, too, notwithstanding the cries of the little ones while we pursued and captured them; she only looking around once, at a distance of half a mile, raising herself on her hind feet in a menacing manner, then again fled rapidly over the hills and disappeared. In the same region, a very large female grizzly defended her young with great desperation, and only fled after the cubs were entirely beyond the reach of the hunters, when she made her escape, covered with wounds.

"The food of these animals, in this country, consists of acorns, walnuts, piñones, (the fruit of the *Pinus edulis*,) manzanillas, the fruit of an ericaceous shrub, and such animals as they are able to capture."—(Dr. Kennerly.)

"*Grizzly bear; oso of the Mexicanos; chas of the Apaches.*—Near the highest crest of the Sierra Madre, called 'San Luis mountains,' I had an opportunity to witness a rare butchery, by which, in less than one hour, a whole family of grizzlies was killed, without one offering the slightest resistance. It was about noon on the 11th of October, 1855, when our long trains, coming from the Guadaloupe Pass, in the Sierra Madre, towards the San Luis springs, met on the plains these unexpected mountaineers. When surprised, they were lying on the ground not far from each other digging roots. The position in which they performed this work naturally caused long narrow strips of grassy lands to be turned up and searched as if it had been done by a bad plough. I could not learn what kind of roots they had been looking for. After taking off the thick skin of these root-diggers, we found them all in a very poor condition, and this may account for the want of that resistance which they failed to offer. The ungrizzly-like behavior of these poor brutes induced the majority of our party to doubt their being grizzlies at all. They evidently had descended from the surrounding mountains, where they have their stronghold in the rough trachytic recesses of this part of the Sierra Madre, the highest crest of which is densely crowned by a dark growth of pines. There their fruit stores had probably given out in the late season, and they were obliged to resort to roots to satisfy their hunger."

24. URSUS CINNAMONEUS, (p. 228,)?—Cinnamon Bear.

? *Ursus americanus*, var. *cinnamomum*, Aud. & Bach. N. A. Quad. III, 1853, 125; pl. cxxvii.

Sp. Ch.—Size equal to or less than that of the black bear. Color various shades of brown, very rarely black. Skull broader than in the common black bear.

Several skulls of a small bear collected by Mr. Clark at the Copper mines of the Gila appear to indicate a species quite different from the common black bear. The animals to which they belonged were all of a distinct brownish color, except one, in which the hair was "glossy black and pretty long." Although about the size of the common black bear, *Ursus americanus*, or a little smaller, yet four skulls of all ages before me, when compared with a corresponding series of seven of *Ursus americanus*, exhibit such characteristic differences as to authorize the conclusion that the species are distinct. Unfortunately none of the skins collected were brought home, owing to difficulty of transportation and other causes, and it is therefore impossible to speak more definitely of the external characters of this bear beyond the color, which was said to be of various shades of brown, with sometimes a reddish tint, sometimes darker, the tips lighter. In these characters it agrees with the cinnamon bear of authors, supposed generally to be a mere variety in color of the common American black bear. There is, however, an essential difference between the two; the cinnamon bear of Oregon being uniform in the color of its hairs from root to tip. Should further comparison show in the cinnamon bear of Oregon the same cranial and other essential characters as the *U. americanus*, differing from the one in question, I should propose the name of *Ursus amblyceps*, in allusion to the great comparative breadth of the head.

I am not aware that any direct comparison has ever been made between the skins and skulls of the black bears of the eastern United States and those of the Rocky mountains and the Pacific slope. It is quite possible that they may be really distinct, and that the western species occurs in the black and brownish varieties, which would substantiate the impression that these two colors in that country belong to one and the same species. There is at any rate no essential difference between the skull of the "black bear" of the Copper mines and the brown bears from the same localities, all exhibiting the same characteristic features as distinguished from the black bear of eastern America. The black variety, however, appears to be much the rarer of the two.

Skull. For reasons already explained I shall select a middle aged skull to serve as the type of my description, and afterwards point out the differences of the very young and very old specimens. Number 994, the head of a female from the Copper mines, has the tubercles of the molars and the crowns of the incisors considerably worn, so as materially to obscure their characteristics, while in a skull of *U. americanus* of the same age the molars are perfectly entire. The sagittal crest extends over a little more than the posterior third of the parietal bone.

The profile of the head exhibits a very decided convex curve from the occiput to the middle of the nasal bones, after which it passes off nearly horizontally, curving downwards towards the tip. The outline is, however, more convex than in *U. americanus*, rising higher in the middle. The central region of the forehead from the coronal suture to the middle of the nasals is nearly plain or slightly convex, rounding off gently on the sides and to the tip of the post-orbital process of the frontal bone.

The outline from above exhibits a much greater breadth between the zygomatic arches than in the skull of black bear described (897), which is, moreover, a little older. Thus the greatest breadth is .617 of the total length, instead of .573. The projection of the end of intermaxillary beyond the end of molar is .316 of the total length; the least width between orbits is .227; the distance between the tips of the orbital processes is .34.

The lower jaw exhibits a decided character in the shape of its coronoid process. In this the upper end curves round into a decided hook, the posterior outline being very much emarginated.

Larger and older specimens exhibit a still greater breadth of head, amounting to as much as .629 hundredths, while still older heads of the black bear are but .597 hundredths.

This species, as already stated, differs very much in the width of the head from *Ursus americanus*; the width of the head being at all ages (except in the very young) more than six-tenths the total length in the one and less than this in the other. The upper edge of the zygomatic arch is a good deal more curved. The lower jaw exhibits a striking character in the great concavity of the hinder edge of the coronoid process, instead of the gentle curve of *U. americanus.*

There is quite an appreciable difference between the two species in reference to the anterior outline of the glenoid cavity. In one these outlines are in the same straight line, while in *U. americanus* they diverge anteriorly, so as to meet at an obtuse angle if produced backwards and inwards.

The molar teeth of *U. cinnamoneus* are much smaller than in *U. americanus*. Thus the three posterior upper molars in the largest specimen of *cinnamoneus* measure but 2.07 inches, the others less than two inches; in the smallest of *americanus* 2.22, in the largest 2.35.

In the description of this species I have not considered it necessary to make any comparisons with the other American bears, the grizzly and the polar, as these vastly surpass it in size. The *Ursus arctos* of Europe is also a much larger animal.

From a comparison of the teeth it is quite evident that the present species is less carnivorous than the *Ursus americanus* of the eastern States. Indeed, its food is said to consist in great part of the piñon or stone pine, and other seeds requiring a considerable amount of grinding before being swallowed.

Skull.	*Ursus cinnamoneus.* ♂. Gila. 991.		*U. cinnamoneus.* ♂ Gila. 992.		*U. americanus.* 988. ♀. Morehouse co., La.	
	Inches.	100ths of length.	Inches.	100ths of length.	Inches.	100ths of length.
Total length	11.50	1.00	11.10	1.00	10.30	1.00
From end of intermaxillaries to end of condyles	10.50	.92	10.60	.95	10.10	.97
Greatest width	6.90	.60	7.00	.63	6.00	.57
Greatest height above base of cranium	3.40	.29	3.20	.28	3.20	.31
Distance between orbits	2.55	.22	2.46	.22	2.30	.22
Distance between orbital processes	3.73	.33	3.63	.32	3.26	.31
Nasal bones, length	2.90	.25	2.90	.26	2.70	.26
Nasal bones, width before	1.14	.09	1.07	.09	1.03	.10
Narrowest part of muzzle behind canines	2.30	.20	2.28	.20	2.23	.20
Upper incisors from front to molars	2.80	.24	2.70	.24	2.30	.22
Upper incisors from front to hinder margin of palate	5.84	.50	5.60	.50	5.37	.52
Upper incisors, width between external edges	1.40	.12	1.45	.13	1.26	.12
Upper molars, length taken together	2.00	.17	2.07	.18	2.24	.21
Upper molars, least distance between	1.57	.13	1.63	.14	1.45	.13
From intermaxillary to end of nasals	4.90	.42	5.28	.47	4.47	.43
From intermaxillary to commencement of orbit	4.17	.36	4.38	.39	3.66	.35
Between post-orbital points to occiput	6.60	.57	6.20	.55	6.00	.58
Between post-orbital points to end of nasals	3.70	.32	3.67	.33	3.40	.33
Between post-orbital points to end of intermaxillary	5.80	.50	6.00	.54	5.10	.49

991. ♂. 992. ♂. 994. ♀. Skulls. Coppermines, N. M. J. H. Clark.

25. DIDELPHYS VIRGINIANA, Shaw, (p. 232.)—Possum.

The under-fur of this species is yellowish white, with dusky tips quite uniformly distributed over the body, most intense on the back. The legs are entirely dusky brown; the digits or fingers and toes yellowish white. The head is nearly pure yellowish white throughout, with only a dusky suffusion round the eye, and a dusky shade along the top of the head, widening and deepening into the brown of the back. The ears are black, with a yellow blotch on the upper edge; the tail is black on the basal fourth, the remainder yellowish white.

The long scattered hairs of the body are quite uniformly distributed and silvery white in color.

Length of head, 5 inches; of head and body, 20½; of tail, 14½.

I am not at present prepared to give the distribution of the common North American possum with any degree of precision. According to Audubon and Bachman its eastern limit is the Hudson river, while westwardly it extends to the Pacific ocean, and southwardly to Mexico. I am, however, inclined to doubt the extent of this range. No evidence is before me of its existence to any great distance west of the Missouri, the south Texas and California species being probably quite different.

This species is not found in southern Texas, but is said to occur in its northeastern portion. I have given its characteristics with the view of illustrating more fully the character of the *D. californica.*

DIDELPHYS CALIFORNICA, Bennett, (p. 233.)—Texas Possum.

This species appears to be considerably smaller than the common possum of the north. The tail is as long as the body, exclusive of the head and neck; the portion covered with hair is only about one-tenth its length.

The ears are large and naked on both sides, higher than wide, and rounded at the tips.

The under-fur is yellowish white throughout, except the terminal portion, which, on the back and sides, is dark brown; nearly black along the middle of the back. This color is more diffused on the sides and beneath. The legs and feet are entirely dusky throughout to the claws. The under part of the head, including the entire lower jaw, is dusky. There is a dusky patch in front of the eye, which commences a little behind the nostril and passes through the eye involving the eyelids, and, extending backwards and curving downwards about as far from the eye as this is from the nose, becomes confluent with the dusky of the chin. There is thus a distinct light patch on the side of the head from the nose, widening behind and terminating in a rounded outline, convex behind. The top of the head is quite dusky, with a faint indication of a dark streak along the central line, the whole confluent with the dusky of the tail. The ears are black, with a yellow blotch in the upper edge. The tail is white, except the basal third, which is black.

The back and side are thickly interspersed with long, yellowish, silvery hairs, thickest along the median line, much scattered on the sides; these measure from two to three inches.

A younger animal (199) is similar to the above in the general pattern of coloration, but is almost entirely black or dark brown throughout, except the light patch on the cheek and one behind the ear. The long, soft hairs are wanting entirely, but the remaining fur is much coarser than in the specimen first described, the hairs black or dark brown, the basal half whitest. There are softer, shorter hairs interspersed, which are black only at the extreme tip.

No. 1058, from the Valley of Mexico, is similar to 138, but rather lighter. The basal half of the tail and the entire ears are black.

This species may be very readily distinguished from the *D. virginiana* by several characters. In the latter species the fingers and toes are white; there is more white on the ear. The head is greyish white, with only a dusky blotch immediately around the eye; but no such pattern of marking as described. The size of *D. virginiana* is considerably larger; its ears more rounded or less pointed above; the hairy portion of the tail longer.

The only other species with which a comparison is required is the *D. azarae.* In this the body is as dark or darker than in the present species; the head and neck are, however, white, with a single central dark stripe along the forehead to the dusky of the nape. The ears and toes are flesh colored. *D. aurita* is similar in some respects, but wants the well defined white cheeks, and has flesh colored toes. *D. cancrivora*, though of dark pelage, has no well defined markings on the head; the long scattered hairs, too, are blackest.

This animal agrees pretty well with the *Didelphys californica* of Bennett, which, however, I cannot distinguish from the *D. breviceps*, except by the length of the tail, which, as given by Bennett, measures 16 inches, with a body of 12. Waterhouse, however, in redescribing the same specimens, gives the head and body at 17 inches; the tail, 14; which is much nearer the proportions of the specimens here described.

The *D. pruinosa*,[1] of Wagner, appears to be the same animal. The *D. californica*, of Burmeister, in Fauna Brasiliens, is described as having the ground color reddish brown.

Although there are some differences in the skulls of the *Didelphys virginiana* and those of the subject of the present article, yet I am not able to establish on them any specific characteristics. In fact, the variations in the thickness and length of the muzzle in different species, in addition to other points, are so great as to readily convey the impression, without a knowledge of the facts, of many more species than really exist. This will be more intelligible from the following measurements:

Measurements of skulls.

	DIDELPHYS VIRGINIANA.								D. CALIFORNICA.			
	2452, Georgia.		2200, Georgia.		680, Carlisle.		527, Carlisle.		1401, Matamoras.		1121, Texas.	
	Inches.	100*ths.*	*Inches.*	100*ths.*	*Inches.*	100*ths.*	*Inches.*	100*ths.*	*Inches.*	100*ths.*	*Inches.*	100*ths.*
Length of skull	5.06	100	4.80	100	4.86	100	3.65	100	4.40	100	3.50	100
Width between zygomata	2.65	52	2.59	52	2.90	60	1.98	54	2.60	59	1.75	50
Distance to orbits	2.19	43	2.10	44	2.18	45	1.61	44	2.05	46	1.55	44
Width of muzzle, behind canine	.98	19	.80	17	1.02	21	.67	18	.96	22	.68	19

Measurements of skins.

Current No.	Locality.	From tip of nose to—				Tail to end of vertebræ.	Length of—		Height of ear above notch.	Nature of specimen.
		Eye.	Ear.	Occip.	Tail.		Fore foot.	Hind foot.		
138	Matamoras			3.80	16.50	11.25	1.50	2.20	1.40	Dry skin
199	Lower Rio Grande				13.00	8.54	1.50	2.10	1.30	....do
1058	City of Mexico	1.52	3.30	3.60	15.50	12.25	1.65	2.20	1.20	....do

1058. City of Mexico. John Potts.—199. Mouth of Rio Grande. J. H. Clark.—1197. Guyapuco, Mexico. Lt. D. N. Couch, U. S. A.—138. Matamoras, Mexico. February, 1853. Lt. D. N. Couch, U. S. A. (26.) Skin.

The range of this species, as shown from the list of specimens, is from Texas to the city of Mexico; how much further cannot now be determined. It probably extends into Upper California, though I have never yet seen any specimens from our Pacific Territory.

"Found on the lower Rio Grande; is not probably an inhabitant of the central part of the continent, as the Mexicans who had come down from Chihuahua had never seen such an animal. Its favorite food is the black persimmon, an abundant fruit of this region."—(J. H. Clark.)

[1] This is quoted by Waterhouse, Burmeister, and others, as described in Wiegmann's Archiv for 1842. The first mention of it by Wagner, however, appears to be in the Suppl. Schreber III, 1843.

ORDER

RODENTIA.

27. SCIURUS LIMITIS, Baird (p. 256.)—Texas Fox Squirrel.

This species is intermediate in size between *S. migratorius* and *carolinensis*, and is quite well characterized by the sparseness of hair everywhere and its compactness; features which we should expect to find in a squirrel from the warmer portions of Texas. There are but four upper molars on each side, all large. The head is broad and rather short; the septum of the nose naked. The ears appear to be unusually high, and coated equally on both sides with very short hairs, without any bushiness or tufts even at the base. The feet are less in their proportions than many other species. The claws, however, are well developed; the fourth finger is longest, the third shorter, the second reaching to the base of the claw of the third and shorter than the fifth, the first or thumb rudimentary, as usual; palms naked. On the hind feet the second, third, and fourth toes are nearly equal; the claw of the fifth reaching a little beyond the base of the claw of the fourth, the first in turn bearing the same relation to the fifth. The sole is naked from the tarsus, (or on the under side of the metatarsus,) a few short hairs only being seen near the outer edge. The inferior surface of the toes is also naked, and without any fringe projecting from the sides. Both palms and soles are dark brown.

As the tip of the tail is broken off, the exact proportions cannot be ascertained; the hairs, however, are rather short and sparse, more scanty than in any other species examined.

As already stated, the hairs everywhere are short; the longest on the back do not measure half an inch, while the average is not more than four lines. The upper parts are a mixed cinnamon and black; the individual hairs being light plumbeous at the base, then cinnamon, then black and tipped with cinnamon brown. The sides of the head, both surfaces of ears, whole under parts, and all the limbs (except the external upper portion) are of a light cinnamon brown, (not rufous,) the hairs being a little lighter towards their bases; the upper surfaces of the feet are tinged with rusty. The hairs on the under surface of the tail are uniform, and of a color a little deeper than that of the belly; those above are like the back, (the color, however, being more yellowish,) with three annulations of black; on the sides they are similarly annulated, with the sub-terminal black more extensive. There is no decided preponderance of color on the upper part and sides of the tail.

A single specimen of this species was obtained by Mr. Clark on Devil's river, or the San Pedro of the Rio Grande, Texas.

Length to base of tail, 10 inches; tail, (multilated,) —; ears above the skull, .60; ears on posterior edge, .75; fore feet from wrist, 1.08; hind feet from heel, 1.67; longest hairs of tail, 2.17; length of skull, 2.25; width of skull between zygomata, 1.30.

Notwithstanding the marked difference in color and size between this species and all the other American fox squirrels, I am far from feeling sure now that it is anything more than a local variety of the common western fox squirrel. Had I deferred characterising the species until the present day, I should hardly have ventured upon a new name without a more ample knowledge of the North American squirrels than I possessed two years ago. I only retain it now provisionally, until its real character can be better tested by additional specimens. The locality is considerably further west than that of any other specimens which have fallen under my notice.

351. Devil's river, Texas. J. H. Clark. J. H. Clark.—1515. Devil's river, Texas. Dr. Kennerly.

"Of this species but a single specimen was seen, and that on Devil's river, in the midst of thick vegetation. It had here built a bed of leaves and twigs, into which it ran on being pursued. After it was forced out of this retreat, and wounded, it took to the ground and attempted to hide in the weeds and grass. This squirrel is said to be quite abundant in eastern Texas, along the margins of rivers where the vegetation is most luxuriant. Its fondness for dense vegetation doubtless explains its ab ence further west. Neither the bark of this nor the preceding species was heard."—(J. H. Clark.)

28. SCIURUS LUDOVICIANUS, Custis. (p. 251.)—Western Fox Squirrel.

Undoubted specimens of this species have been found in eastern Texas.

29. SCIURUS CAROLINENSIS, ? ?. (p. 263.)—Mexican Grey Squirrel.

In the collection of Lieutenant Couch are two grey squirrels from Santa Catarina, New Leon, which differ from the common grey squirrel of the United States in some quite appreciable points. They are smaller, with longer tail, and shorter and broader feet. The hair is coarser, above more decidedly grey and black, beneath very pure white, without any indication of the rusty line on the side of the belly, seldom if ever wanting in the more northern grey squirrels.

The skull differs from that of the common grey squirrel in lacking the small anterior upper molar, leaving but four, as in the fox squirrel. The zygoma extends further backwards, the muzzle shorter and broader. The nasal bones have their edges nearly parallel for the posterior third, instead of approaching each other gently behind.

Some skulls from San Antonio, Texas, (without skins,) agree in character with the above; one out of three has the small anterior molar.

30. SCIURUS CASTANONOTUS, Baird (p. 206.)—Chestnut-backed Squirrel.

This large and stoutly built squirrel belongs to the section with five permanent molars in the upper jaw. Of two skulls before me, one, No. 1108, shows the two anterior permanent molars just appearing, the temporary ones having been shed; the three posterior have their crowns perfectly unworn. There is also a very small rudimentary fifth anterior molar in the lower jaw, which may, however, be the remnant of the deciduous premolar. In another, No. 1107, the five permanent molars are all in place, with the crowns somewhat worn; the entire fifth molar of the lower jaw has disappeared. These skulls exhibit a somewhat greater prominence than usual of the anterior portion.

The whiskers are black and longer than the head. The ears are high and not at all tufted, although the hairs are moderately long on the anterior inflected portion. The feet are moderate; the third and fourth fingers equal and longest; the second and fifth about equal; their claws reaching the claws of the others; the thumb or first, as usual, is rudimentary. The fourth, third, and second toes are successively a little shorter, but longest of all; the fifth reaches to the claw of the fourth, and the first to that of the fifth; the soles are naked from the tarsus, (or on the under surface of the metatarsus,) although the hairs encroach somewhat on the outer edge.

The tail is a little longer than the body. It is not bushy, but rather slender, and the hairs are not full, as in most of the other large species.

The general tint of the upper parts and sides of the body and limbs is a mixed lead color and ash grey, with some scattered black hairs. The whole back from the nape to the base of the tail is of a deep and well-defined chestnut brown; this color being not a mere dorsal stripe, but covering a space the width of the tail. The sides of the head and the ears are grizzled ash. The under parts, the eyelids, and the upper surfaces of the feet are of a rather clear white, the latter somewhat grizzled. The colors of the sides and belly are separated by a dusky line, as in the chickarees. There are some scattered chestnut hairs in the sides. The tail is entirely white and black; the central portion black above, white beneath, with white margin and tip; but all the black hairs are tipped with white. The hairs of the tail beneath are uniform white; on the sides they are mostly white, mixed with a few black ones; on the upper portion they are black at the base, then white, then black and tipped with white, the black predominating. In one specimen, however, the supra-caudal hairs are glossy black, except at their tips, which is the case in both with the hairs at the end of the tail.

Two specimens, male and female, of this species were collected by Mr. Clark at the Copper mines of the Gila, in the spring season. They were found among the pines.

Length to root of tail, 12; tail to end of vertebrae, 11; tail to end of hairs, 12.75; greatest width of tail, hairs extended, 4 50; hind feet from heel, 2.60; hind feet, naked part of soles, 2.08; height of ear above skull, .84; height of ear behind, 1.33; length of skull, 2.40; breadth across zygomata, 1.33.

This species bears a very close resemblance to *S. aberti*, and may prove to be the same, although there are apparent differences. The most striking characteristic is the absence of the beautiful ear tufts of *S. aberti*. Some of our squirrels which have smooth ears in summer are tufted in winter, but as the Copper mine specimens were caught in spring, it is not likely that they are ever tufted. The tufts, too, of *S. aberti* are long hairs growing from the very margins of the ears and project an inch beyond. The interior surface of the ear and a wooly space at their posterior bases are greyish white in *S. castanonotus*. Great differences again are visible in the tail, which in the latter is nearly pure black and white; the inferior hairs pure white, those on the upper surface and upper part of the sides are black, with white tips, greyish at the base. In *S. aberti* all the hairs above are annulated several times with dark brown and greyish white, presenting no decided impression of either color, except towards the end of the tail. The tail here is likewise much more bushy.

S. fossor is without the dorsal stripe and the dark lateral line. The tail is much fuller and more bushy; the hairs beneath the tail are finely annulated ash grey and black, without any of them being entirely white. The feet also are dark colored.

The skull of this species is of very nearly the same size with that of *S. carolinensis*, from Carlisle. Like this species it has an anterior small upper molar, making five, but this is considerably larger in the New Mexican animal, and has a central tubercle on the crown, with a lateral valley on either side, as in the spermophile. There are no other differences of importance.

The name of *castanotus*, as originally published, was a typographical error, not detected until too late, and conveys an erroneous impression in regard to the color of the ears.

121. 122. Copper mines of the Mimbres, N. M. Winter? 1857. J. H. Clark.

"This squirrel was observed in greatest abundance among the tall pines growing on the mountains about the Copper mines. Though the piñon (the fruit of this pine) at seasons constitutes its principal and almost only food, it frequents the ground; on being alarmed it seeks the largest trees, and hides itself in the topmost branches, without ever showing any disposition to leap from tree to tree. That it always sought safety in the nearest large tree when surprised led me to believe that it does not resort habitually to 'hollows," but lives and rears its young in 'nests.' Although occuring in greatest numbers in pine regions, it was occasionally met with among the oak-covered mountains about Santa Cruz."—(J. H. Clark.)

31. TAMIAS DORSALIS, Baird (p. 300)—Gila Striped Squirrel.

Head acutely pointed; body elongated; feet and limbs moderately developed. Thumb rudimentary, with a nail; third and fourth toes and claws equal; second a little shorter than the fifth or exterior, the claw of which reaches to the base of that of the third. Palms naked. On the hind feet the inner toe is shortest; the second, third, and fourth successively longer; the fifth claw reaches a little beyond the base of the fourth. Sole naked or with a few scattered hairs; heel hairy. Claws all well developed, and clothed with bristles at the base. Tail quite short, little more than half the length of body.

This species has the lines on the sides of the face, as in other species of *Tamias*, but they are better defined than usual. Thus there is a distinct line nearly white from the snout over the eye, but not extending to the ear. A branch passes under the eye, and, extending beneath and along the base of the ear, is lost in a hoary patch behind it. A dark reddish brown stripe, mixed with black, separates the upper stripe from the crown, and another similar to it divides the lower stripe throughout its length from the dirty white of the throat and neck. A third line of the same passes back from the eye to the base of the ear, and runs up on the anterior inflected portion, where, however, it is nearly pure reddish brown.

The ears, as stated, are reddish brown on the anterior third; another third is greyish brown; the rest or posterior portion is dirty greyish white, continuous with a patch of the same behind the ear, and extending backwards for half an inch. The concavity of the ear is well covered with short hairs; brownish anteriorly, ferruginous on the posterior half.

The especial characteristic of this species is seen in the single well defined dorsal stripe of dark brown, extending from the back of the head where it distinctly separates the hoary patches already mentioned, and extends to the base of the tail. On either flank is visible a faint line of light greyish, occupying the position of the exterior light line of other species of *Tamias*. There are also the faintest possible traces of the other dark and light lines, making up the five dark and four light stripes of *Tamias*. The top of the head and upper parts generally have in general a hoary or greyish aspect, mixed with light reddish and brown; the former predominating in one specimen, the latter in another. The under parts are dull greyish white; the sides of the body, the buttocks and the exterior surfaces of the hind feet pale rusty, lighter on the fore feet.

The tail is more bushy than usual. On the upper surface the hairs are glossy black at the base, then chestnut, then black, and finally dull white; the first two colors of equal extent, about half that of the two latter. Beneath the hairs are chestnut at the base.

Two specimens of this distinctly marked species were procured at Fort Webster, Copper mines (where it is rare), in the winter of 1851.

Measurements.—Total length, 5 inches; tail vertebrae, 2; tail to tip, 3.50; hairs of tail at tip, 1.50; hairs on sides, 1.25; hind foot from heel, 1.25.

This species is readily distinguished from all others by the single dorsal stripe, the others being obsolete. The more bushy tail, with its conspicuous markings of chestnut black and white, is also highly characteristic of it.

119, 120. Fort Webster, Copper mines of the Mimbres, N. M. Winter? 1857. J. H. Clark. Skin.

"This was found only about the cañons in the Copper mine region. It is secluded in its habits, and never wanders far from its abode, which seemed to be principally in the crevices of rocks. Once one was run into a hollow cedar; but this only proved to be a temporary or rural habitation, for, on the first jar of the tree, it ran out and made for the rocks. Aware of its presence in a certain cañon during my stay at the Copper mines, its shyness and seclusion for a long time baffled my utmost efforts to secure a specimen. I finally adopted the plan of 'lying in wait,' which proved successful in this, as in many other cases. After watching for some hours there was a shower of rain, when some three or four cautiously emerged from a crevice dripping wet; rain, being an unusual thing, probably took them by surprise. While combing their hair with their paws and licking themselves dry, one shot secured three. Piñons, cedar berries, and acorns are its food."—(J. H Clark.)

32. SPERMOPHILUS GRAMMURUS, Bach. (p. 310.)—Line-tailed Squirrel.

125, 126. Copper mines, N. M. J. H. Clark.—? 1046. Los Nogales, Sonora. June, 1855. Dr. Kennerly.

"This very squirrel-like spermophile was observed in great numbers in the neighborhood of the Copper mines. Thence westward it inhabits the mountainous regions; its occurrence east of the Rio Grande is doubtful. Its home is between and under the strata of rock; it sometimes, however, apparently burrows directly into the side of the mountain, and to a great depth, judging from the amount of dirt brought out. On examination these holes were found to lead along the face of the rocks, probably because the soil is here looser and more easily moved.

"Several sometimes inhabit the same locality, but it is more frequently seen alone. At the Copper mines, where I had a good opportunity of studying the habits and manners of this and other animals, it seemed to select its retreat with reference to food, acorns and walnuts, for which it climbs the trees, and with great facility, but always hastily leaves them when alarmed, and hies away to near its hole, where it stops to reconnoitre. If its suspicions are well founded, it dodges in, but usually comes out again in a few minutes and returns to its labor or amusement above ground. Early in the morning or late in the evening, may most always be seen about its den, feeding or playing; about mid-day, as if following the example set by the 'lords of creation' that dwell here, it retires for a siesta. The pouches of the specimens obtained were filled with acorns in process of transportation for winter store. Occasionally one may be heard, while sitting at the entrance of his house, uttering a short, sharp note. I could never make out whether this bark was the wail of distress or the call of companionship; it always proceeded from an isolated and lonely individual."—(J. H. Clark.)

"We first observed this species (No. 1046) in the Santa Cruz mountains, and afterwards found it very common in the vicinity of Los Nogales. It seemed to make its nest indifferently in the rocks or in hollow trees, when there was an entrance about the root, but we have very seldom seen it climb the trees. In its movements on the ground it very closely resembled the common grey squirrel (*Sciurus carolinensis*), perhaps not so swift and active. It walked leisurely from point to point while searching for food, and rarely leaped and jumped like the latter, though it often paused, raised itself on its hind legs, and seemed to listen and reconnoitre. It was quite shy, and was never found far from its den, to which it rapidly fled upon the slightest appearance of danger.

"Its food consisted principally of acorns, of which there were generally an abundance in the regions where it was found."—(Dr. Kennerly.)

33. SPERMOPHILUS COUCHII, Baird (p. 311.)—Black Ground Squirrel.

338. Santa Caterina, N. Leon. April, 1853. Lt. Couch.

34. SPERMOPHILUS TERETICAUDA, Baird (p. 316.)—Round-tailed Spermophile.

1584. ♂. Fort Yuma, Cal. Maj. G. H. Thomas, U. S. A. Skin.

35. SPERMOPHILUS MEXICANUS, Wagner. (p. 319.)—Mexican Ground Squirrel.

This well kown spermophile is found probably throughout Mexico, although the Rio Grande appears to be about its northern limit. It is found as far west as the Pecos, and even at El Paso, where, however, it begins to be replaced by *S. spilosoma*, which in turn extends to the Gulf of California.

518. Pesquièra Grande, Mex. May, 1853. Lt. D. N. Couch, U. S. A. 203.—2498. Matamoras, Mex. May, 1853. Lt. D. N. Couch, U. S. A.—352. Brownsville, Tex. Feb., 1853. Lt. D. N. Couch, U. S. A.—140. Eagle Pass, Tex. 1852. A. Schott.

"This species was found in greatest numbers in the valley of the lower Rio Grande. It lives in the ground, and its burrow is always made with reference to the protection afforded by a thorny brush or cacti against the attacks of the coyote and other enemies. If the entrance happens to be in an exposed place, it is sometimes fortified by thorny pieces of the mesquite and cacti. Though somewhat companionable, each, as a rule, seems to have its own house. Like other mammals, it is most above ground in the morning and evening in search of food ; yet it is apparently the least affected by the heat of the midday sun. It is omnivorous. Its bed is a globular mass, lined with soft material, and has but one entrance."—(J. H. Clark.)

36. SPERMOPHILUS SPILOSOMA, Bennett (p. 321.)—Sonora Ground Squirrel.

This species was first described by Bennett from a specimen obtained in western Mexico. It occurs abundantly from the Gulf of California as far east as El Paso, and even northward to Fort Stanton.

290. Chihuahua city. 1853. John Potts.—1042. Janos, Sonora. April, 1855. Dr. Kennerly.—141. ♀. El Paso. 1852. J. H. Clark.

"This species was quite common on the prairies around Janos. It lived sometimes among the rocks, but more often had its bed in piles of dirt heaped around the base of some bush. These piles were elevated several feet above the surrounding ground, and were entered by three, four, or more apertures near its summit. They were exceedingly shy, and a specimen was procured with difficulty."—(Dr. Kennerly.)

37. CYNOMYS LUDOVICIANUS, Baird (p. 331.)—Prairie Dog.

The well known prairie dog is an inhabitant of the central portions of the United States, from the Upper Missouri region to the Rio Grande. It has not yet been found west of the Rocky mountains, unless a young animal, possibly of this species, collected by Dr. Kennerly between Janos and San Luis Spring, may be considered as indicating this fact.

1054. Devil's river, Tex. Dr. C. B. Kennerly.—1035. ○. San Luis Spring. April, 1855. J. H. Clark.—161. Limpio Mts. J. H. Clark.—498. San Antonio to El Paso. J. H. Clark.

"This animal is well known under the name of 'prairie dog,' and as almost the only inhabitant of the high dry prairie land, destitute of every form of vegetation except grass. The pursley (*Portulacca*) is a favorite food ; in the most populous parts of their towns, after having eaten up the grass to the very roots, they migrate to a more verdant spot. In extensive towns of old standing there is sometimes scarcely a sprig of grass to be seen for miles. They prefer the depressions or hollows in the prairies, partly because of the greater amount of vegetation in such places, but also because of the reservoirs of water that are probably collected here. When the water has wholly evaporated, or sunk below their reach, as sometimes must be the case, the succulent roots supply its place. Whether the result of instinct or a rational deduction, their habit certainly comes under the motto of 'early to bed and early to rise ;" for little is seen or heard of them after sunset ; and before sunrise they are seen in great numbers and all sizes, feeding, chasing each other, or sitting on their haunches ; they frequently assume this latter position when approached. As the sun heightens and it becomes hot they disappear in their burrows, till, in the heat of the day, there is scarcely one to be seen. When it rains they come out in great numbers, pile dirt around the entrance to their holes, which are sometimes completely covered over, presenting the appearance of a dutch oven in minature. In closing up their burrows, they mix grass with the mud and work from the inside after it is nearly completed. There is no doubt that this is done with the object of securing themselves against the water that may collect or run through the depressions in the prairie which they inhabit. once witnessed, near Presidio del Norte, the 'drowning out' of a small town by a sudden and heavy shower; some swam to the high ground, many were drowned, and not a few fell a prey to the coyote. Several were taken alive and kept a month; they were fed on pursely, of which they ate voraciously; they also drank water freely. Most of the time, however, they lay on their bellies in a sort of stupor, with their nose and feet drawn together. A prairie dog is always fat; and, under some circumstances, may be considered good eating; which, being deposited in a comparative great quantity between the skin and muscle, renders the skinning a tedious operation. Their burrows, at first either nearly perpendicular or slightly inclined for a few feet, lead off in various directions; their extent I was never able to ascertain. Half a dozen or more will at times run into the same burrow; yet they will pass, even when hotly pursued, very eligible habitations externally, showing, though eminently social, that each has his own house. In all discussions of the prairie dog it has been universally associated with the owl and the rattlesnake, and for no very good reason that I see. The rattlesnake is found in other localities just as abundant as in dog towns; and if one is seen in or about a burrow, a close examination is very apt to disclose a spider's web across the entrance, indicating that the rightful occupant has been frightened off or devoured. The owl is undoubtedly an interloper, using its neighbor's house as a convenience, and possibly feeding upon its young; its proximity, however, gives the dog no uneasiness, and both inhabit the same burrow at the same time."—(J. H. Clark.)

"This interesting little animal, about which so much has already been written, and its habits so closely studied and accurately described by many naturalists, never fails to attract the attention of every traveller on the western prairies; and an approach to one of their settlements, after long and dreary marches, is always hailed with delight as a pleasant change from the monotony of lifeless scenes to one of cheerful activity and motion. Such occasions never fail to excite a certain degree of pleasure in every one, as he watches the motions of these curious creatures as they at first assemble in numbers as if in grave consultation in regard to the intrusion of strangers upon their quiet domain, and, upon the too near approach of apparent danger, suddenly the assembly is dispersed, each one retiring to his respective home, and, standing upon the edge of his den, utters his peculiar bark, as if in defiance; and then every one disappears suddenly, and every voice is hushed when a single gun is discharged.

"These settlements or 'dog towns,' as they are called, are of frequent occurrence between Devil's river, of Texas, and the Rio Grande, some of them covering many miles of country. West of the latter stream we observed them as far as the Sierra Madre. We visited the San Luis valley in the month of May, where there was a very large extent of country covered with their burrows. Here we procured a young one, which was probably a week or two old. We were attracted to it by a low whining noise which it made, not unlike that of a very young kitten. It was found on the surface, and was so young and feeble that it did not attempt to escape when approached. Having taken it to the camp, we placed it with a bitch, which had pupped but a few days before. By holding it in our hands it sucked with great earnestness, and we much hoped thus to be enabled to rear it and tame it; but after some days it sickened, and, refusing to take farther nourishment, soon died. After leaving this valley, in travelling westward, we did not again observe the 'prairie dog.'"—(Dr. Kennerly.)

The prairie dog of the Americans; perrito del campo of the Mexican; tlui of the Apaches.—This singular animal is known to all western travellers, but there are some features in its history still left to be elucidated. Do they wander, and, if so, is it in a certain direction? If they remain stationary, what do they live on? Are the rattlesnake and the smaller ground-owl (*Athene hypugaea*) constant house-mates of the prairie dog? If so, what object makes such heterogenous animals live together?

There are not yet enough data on record to answer these questions conclusively; on the contrary, every attempt to do so proves only how little we know about them. That the dog towns should be entirely permanent seems to be an entire impossibility, for the destruction of vegetation, which such a marmot settlement causes all around, is so complete that nothing is left within the limits of it on which these animals could depend for any length of time.

"From what I have seen of these marmot settlements, I believe that, after one stretch of soil is used up, an adjacent portion on either side is taken possession of. The social character of the animal causes this to be done *en masse*, and thus the town will be extended in some direction. It seems not probable that the prairie dogs abandon their settlement entirely; this is at least not corroborated by careful examination. Their burrows are the only defense these animals have, and therefore they never dare leave them at a great distance. They want their holes near by where they feed. Long drought and sterility favor the extension of their towns."—(A. Schott.)

38. CASTOR CANADENSIS, Kuhl (p. 355.)—American Beaver.

This well known species was found in abundance on the Rio Grande of Texas and the Colorado river of California.

1337. Colorado Bottom, Cal. A. Schott.—1003. Upper Rio Grande. J. H. Clark.—1415. Matamoras, Mex. Dr. Berlandiere. Skull.

The beaver; pen of the Yumas; pin of the Cocapas.—The abundance of this species on the Gila, but especially on the Colorado del Oeste, makes it a very prominent feature in the fauna of the country. On a reconnoisance down the latter river to its mouth, we passed miles and miles of river banks, which are inhabited, fortified, and covered over by the labor of this singular animal.

We had, however, no opportunity of observing any of that celebrated, almost miraculous, regularity and ingenuity with which, according to general belief, the dens and dams of the beaver are constructed.

Like the aerial nest of the Colorado tree rat or the amphibiously placed stronghold of the muskrat, the beaver's dwelling-place forms also a chaotic heap of drift wood, rush, and mud.

In those nests which have come under our eyes, only one hole communicating with the out and inside could be observed. Whether there are more, and especially sub-fluviatile openings, I am not able to say, though I doubt it, according to what I have seen of beaver life. Of that celebrated ingenuity and those architectural efforts of the beaver I could not learn any particulars. All the skill exhibited in erecting and locating those huts prove but a certain amount of instinct, of which many other mammals possess a similar share, and in which especially birds and insects are far ahead.

The most elevated point on our boundary line where beaver life came to our knowledge is the Guadaloupe cañon, (Sierra Madre,) about 5, 000 feet above salt water. The lowest beaver habitation was seen by ourselves, about 30 miles above the mouth of the Colorado, where the last timber gives way to those unbounded cane-brakes and salt marshes which border the head of the Californian Gulf.

39. GEOMYS CLARKII, Baird, (p. 383.) Pecos Gopher.

This species thus far has only been found near Presidio del Norte and on the Pecos river, where several specimens were obtained.

6. Presidio del Norte. Major W. H. Emory. Skin. J. H. Clark.

40. THOMOMYS UMBRINUS, Baird, (p. 399.)—Sonora Gopher.

If I am correct in the identification, this species was first described from a specimen collected at "Cadadaiguias, Louisiana," a locality of which I can at the present day find no trace. It appears to be quite abundant in New Mexico and Sonora, although its precise range is not yet well ascertained.

154. Fort Webster. J. H. Clark. Skin. J. H. Clark.—149. Santa Cruz, Sonora. Skin. J. H. Clark.—1036. Espia, Sonora. Skin. Dr. Kennerly.—?1331. Santa Isabel, California. November 26, 1854. Skin. A. Schott.

"Though traces of this animal may be often seen in the alluvial soil of the mountain valleys in northern Mexico, it is very inconspicuous itself, being nocturnal. It seldom exposes the whole of its body above ground in daylight. On coming to the surface, if the grass is sufficiently near to be reached, it seizes a sprig and drags it within the entrance, and with its fore feet packs it away in its pouches; when this operation is completed, the opening is filled up with loose earth, which has been aptly described by suggesting its resemblance to the "emptied contents of a flower-pot." If there is no grass near its opening, it will sometimes come entirely out, when it can be easily bewildered and captured. The surface gives way under the foot where this pouched rat has been at work; it is not the species, however, that burrows so extensively in the prairie and piles up the large hollow mounds, the cause of many an inward curse to the inexperienced traveller "[1]—(J. H. Clark.)

"This animal had its hole on a grassy spot on the bank of the Corralitas river. For several successive mornings before sunrise it was observed to come cautiously out to gather grass and roots, and carry them into his den, never, however, venturing more than a few feet from the entrance. It seemed always to be uneasy and apprehensive of danger, and at the slighest noise or motion on our part it immediately disappeared, after the lapse of some time returning, first protruding its head and reconnoitering. When it was killed its pouches were filled with grass, but the manner in which it was put there could not be seen. The hole in which it lived was perfectly smooth, and did not go straight down, but inclined considerably, and apparently did not extend far beneath the surface. Near by was a pile of dirt which had probably been removed from it."—(Dr. Kennerly.)

41. THOMOMYS FULVUS, Baird, (p. 402.)

This species was first obtained by Dr. Woodhouse in the San Francisco mountains of New Mexico, and appears to be confined to the regions west of the Rocky mountains.

1330. Fort Yuma, California. January 2, 1855. A. Schott.

[1] These remarks may possibly apply to the *Geomys clarkii*.

"The specimen of our collection was obtained on the sandy banks of the Colorado, not far below Fort Yuma. I found it slowly moving upon the drifting sand between the river thickets formed by willows, cotton trees, bacharis, and tessaria. As it did not seem to notice much my approach, I concluded that this animal must be weak-sighted in daylight and probably nocturnal in its habits."—(A. Schott.)

42. DIPODOMYS ORDII, Woodhouse, (p. 410.)—Kangaroo Rat.

This species was first described by Dr. Woodhouse from specimens collected at El Paso, the same locality as that of the boundary collections.

560. El Paso, Texas. J. H. Clark.—1044. Mesilla valley. 1855. Dr. Kennerly.—143. Santa Cruz, Sonora. J. H. Clark.—372. Durango, Mexico. Dr. T. H. Webb.

"This species inhabits loose or sandy soil habitually, where may be seen piles of dirt of an oval shape scattered here and there each of which would fill a cart. These heaps of dirt are hollow, and have several entrances about the base, which are much larger than the animal. Sometimes, after the habitation seems to be completed, the dirt is brought out of these holes and deposited at a distance of several yards. Their labor is done almost entirely at night, and they are but seldom seen by daylight. The piles of dirt readily give way under the foot, and a mule or horse will shrink from them with as much fear as they do from a rattlesnake. I could never succeed in frightening out the occupants by running sticks into the entrances or knocking the heaps in. Rattlesnakes are often seen in the holes, which form a constant and secure retreat for all the lizards "—(J. H. Clark.)

43. DIPODOMYS AGILIS, Gambel, (p. 414.)

It is with some hesitation that I refer the specimens collected by Mr. Schott to this species, as they are too young to furnish any very satisfactory indications.

1348. Fort Yuma, California. In alcohol. A. Schott.

44. PEROGNATHUS PENICILLATUS, Woodhouse, (p. 418.)

1332. Colorado river. February 22, 1855. A. Schott.—1333. Fort Yuma. A. Schott.—Colorado desert. In alcohol. A. Schott.

45. PEROGNATHUS HISPIDUS, Baird. (p. 421.)

Of this species several specimens were collected at Matamoras, and it probably extends further north into Texas.

577. Charco Escondido, and 576. Matamoras, Mex. Lt. Couch.

46. PEROGNATHUS FLAVUS, Baird. (p. 423.)

This species is found quite abundantly throughout the west, from the lower Rio Grande to El Paso, and a considerable distance westward. It also extends through the Rocky mountains to he Missouri river.

1043. San Antonio to El Paso. Major Emory. In alcohol. Dr. C. B. Kennerly.—1041. El Paso to Los Nogales. In alcohol. Dr. C. B. Kennerly.—148. El Paso. 1851. Col. Graham. J. H. Clark.—2623. Chihuahua. Dr. T. H. Webb.

47. MUS TECTORUM, Savi. (p. 441.)—White-bellied Rat; Roof Rat.

Of this species of rat, specimens were collected at Cadereita, New Leon, by Lt. Couch, and skulls, apparently of the same species, are in the Berlandier collection from Matamoras.

"The people of the neighborhood of Fort Duncan talk of a three years' cyclus, during which the appearance of hundred thousands of rats is repeated once. According to the description given to me, I think the animal to be of the species above mentioned.

"Some of the soldiers who had been engaged in making the excavations for the groundworks of some of the buildings during one of these 'rat years' told me that they could easily kill every morning from thirty to forty of these rats, which had descended or tumbled down into these diggings without being able to scale again the vertical walls.

"According to further statements these animals seem to disappear again suddenly, after which hundreds and thousands can be found lying dead over the surrounding table lands. The decaying matter then renders the infected atmosphere almost insufferable."—(A. Schott.)

48. REITHRODON MEGALOTIS, Baird. (p. 451)

Sp. Ch. Largest of North American species. Head and body from 2.50 to 3 inches; tail about two-tenths shorter. Hind foot near .70. Ears large, moderately clothed with hair. Above mouse gray, lined with darker, and tinged with rusty; on the rump and sides a fulvous wash. Beneath soiled yellowish white.

Two specimens of *Reithrodon* were collected by Dr. Kennerly between Janos, Sonora, and San Luis spring, which I cannot readily refer to any of the described North American species. In size they exceed any of their congeners in the United States, being nearly as large as a *Hesperomys*. The ears are conspicuously large and broad, projecting far beyond the fur. They are not so thick as in *R. montanus*, and not quite so thickly clothed with hair; more so than in *R. lecontii*. The hind feet are moderately long; soles hairy to the first tubercles. The tail is about as long as the body, exclusive of the head; it is well clothed with hairs, concealing the annuli.

The upper parts are somewhat of a mouse color, lined with darker, and with a rusty tinge on the rump and sides; this is tinged with fulvous. The under parts and feet are of a soiled yellowish white. This animal has a much shorter tail than the California species. The ears are considerably larger than in *R. montanus* and *lecontii.*

1039. Janos to San Luis spring. Mounted. Dr. Kennerly.

49. HESPEROMYS TEXANUS, Woodhouse. (p. 464.)

This species is so closely allied to the *H. leucopus* as to be distinguished with difficulty.

?145. El Paso, Texas. Col. Graham. Skin. J. H. Clark.—1037. Turkey creek, Texas. Nov., 1854. Major Emory. Dr. C. B. Kennerly.—579. Charco Escondido, Mex. Lieut. Couch. Skin.

"In passing through a groove of live oaks (*Quercus virens*) in the valley of Turkey creek, late in the afternoon, we observed near the top of one of the trees a nest built of leaves closely resembling those sometimes constructed by the common Carolina squirrel. Being desirous of ascertaining whether there was any animal in the nest we discharged our rifle at it, which resulted in the two mice presented being dislodged from it. We knew of no reason why, in this locality, they should have abandoned the usual habits of their kind, and selected this position instead of building their nest in the ground, under stones, or in old logs."—(Dr. Kennerly.)

50. HESPEROMYS SONORIENSIS, Leconte, (p. 474.)

144. Santa Cruz, Sonora. 1851. J. H. Clark.—9. El Paso, Texas. J. H. Clark.

"This animal seems to live, as circumstances may determine, either in the ground or in the hollows of trees. A specimen obtained from a 'hollow' of a cottonwood tree had a snug bed made of the fine filaments or inside bark; in this there was apparently no provision made for a family, or even for a companion. This seclusion is not probably peculiar to the genus but only the freak of a disgusted or selfish individual.

"This, or an allied species, builds globular beds of fine grass, lined with feathers and other soft material, on the Opuntia and other chapparel. They are quite numerous in some sections, and, seen at a distance, hanging on thorny branches, resemble old bird nests. The entrance, usually at the side or bottom, is, to all appearance, so entirely closed as to suggest the question, by what built, and for what purpose is such a contrivance? I never saw one in an unfinished state, nor the animal at work—labor is perhaps performed after night."—(J. H. Clark.)

51. HESPEROMYS EREMICUS, Baird (p. 479.)—Desert Mouse.

This strongly marked species has hitherto only been found at Fort Yuma and its vicinity.

1334. Colorado Bottom, Cal. A. Schott.

52. NEOTOMA MEXICANA Baird (p. 490.)—Bush Rat.

1033. San Pedro R., Sonora. Dr. Kennerly.—1328. ♂ Colorado bottom, Cal. March 31, 1855. A. Schott.

"The only specimen of this species observed by me was procured near the San Pedro river on a bluff, where it had built its nest among the rocks. Evidences of its presence were perceived in great quantities of excrement around the spot; and, after removing a few stones, its nest was found, and the animal easily captured. The nest was composed of a compact bunch of dry grass.

"The food of this animal consists partly, perhaps, of the cactus and its fruit, which grew in abundance in this locality."—(Dr. Kennerly.)

"*Raton of the Mexicans; Lotronce, of the Apaches; Amalj, of the Yumas.*

"This animal is most common in the bottom lands of the Lower Colorado, and most probably in corresponding localities on the Gila.

"It builds its domicile between the forks of mezquite trees, the deflexed ramifications of which usually form a natural defence against larger intruders. The nest itself is made up of dry sticks, such as the ground underneath such trees is strewn with. There is no regularity in the construction of this house, which resembles, on a smaller scale, those of the beavers. The only difference is, that the rat builds his house above freshet-mark. As a common inmate of those rat nests is also a *Sceleporus*, perhaps, *Sc. collaris*, which has its entomophagous sports upon the rough bark of the mezquite tree. Thus the rat and the lizzard live peaceably together.

"The principal food of this rat seems to be the pods of the mezquite and the screw bean, of which often large depositories can be found in their strongholds.

"The animal seems to avoid carefully any contact with water, and therefore likes to build its nest above the reach of water. Being obliged to live for some months on deposited food, its habitation necessarily must remain perfectly dry.

"For the Indians, Yumas and Cocopas, living in the Colorado bottom, this tree rat is of some importance. As they do not hunt, they depend on the meat of this rat for that small portion of animal food they want. In spring, that is, in February and March, the rat nests are carefully searched by the Indians. It was in this season that when, after some of us had refused the offer of an Indian to sell us some of this delicacy, he assured us in his peculiar Indian-Spanish, 'mucho bueno por comer;' and then went to my camp-fire, and, after killing one or two of his long-tailed prisoners, placed it, without any cleaning, into hot ashes. After a quarter of an hour the dish was ready, and required only a little salt to make it palatable to the native consumer."—(A. Schott.)

53. NEOTOMA MICROPUS, Baird (p. 492.)—Black Wood Rat.

554. Charco Escondido. Mexico. 1853. Lt. D. N. Couch.—561. Santa Rosalio, Mexico. Lt. Couch.

54. SIGMODON BERLANDIERI, Baird (p. 504.)—Texas Cotton Rat.

8. West of San Antonio. Skin. J. H. Clark.—233. Eastern Texas. Skin. J. H. Clark.—2682. Ringgold Barracks. A. Schott.—1034. Los Nogales, Sonora. Dr. Kennerly.

"It sometimes inhabits the vicinity of water courses, seeking the tufts of grass usually growing here as a place of retreat. It also burrows into river bluffs and banks of ravines; its burrows, however, are more properly some sun-cracked crevice or water-washed hole, which is apparently selected at times with reference to some adjacent rank vegetation. Sticks, feathers, and other foreign matter are collected about its habitation, which is otherwise marked by clean and well beaten paths, sometimes forming a sort of tunnel through leaves and fallen weeds and grass. Like the Norway rat, it seems to be omnivorous, and is a day as well as a night feeder. The specimens obtained were shot as they skipped from one cover to another."—(J. H. Clark.)

"This species was quite common at Los Nogales, but we did not observe it in any other locality. It lived in the ground, in the immediate valley of the stream where the soil was of a soft alluvial character. It frequented the places occupied by the cooks, and its depredations often amounted to annoyances. It was not entirely nocturnal in its habits, but frequently made its appearance during the day time, and was not very shy."—(Dr. Kennerly.)

55. FIBER ZIBETHICUS, Cuv. (p. 561.)—Musk Rat.

No specimens of this species were collected by any member of the commission.

"During my whole journey along the boundary line I only saw one specimen of this interesting genus. It was killed in the low marshes of the Gila, near Fort Yuma. The ball had taken off the animal's head entirely.

"To conclude from the number of tracks we saw on the Gila and Colorado, and also on the Rio Bravo, the Ondatra cannot by any means be rare.

"In one nest which we accidentally opened in the bottom of the Colorado, and supposed to be the habitation of a musk rat, we found a large store of screw beans, on which the animal seems to feed in winter time."—(A. Schott.)

56. LEPUS CALLOTIS, Wagler (p. 590.)—Jackass Rabbit; Texas Hare.

Sp. Ch.—Size large; limbs very long. Ears much longer than the head. Fur variable; fuller in winter and on high table lands, thinner in summer. The dorsal region mixed reddish yellow or light cinnamon and black; the hairs grayish white at the base; sides and fore part of chest and throat paler, with much less black; buttocks, sides of the rump, and external surface of hind legs ash gray, finely and faintly lined with dark brown, which, on the buttocks, appears arranged in lines somewhat parallel to the outline of the longer fur of the back; upper surface of the tail, with a line on the rump, black; rest of the tail ash gray; beneath, smoked white. Ears, with the posterior edge, white; this color also visible on the interior face of the ear, except the external band, which, with the internal, is grizzled pale cinnamon yellow and brown; end of the ear with a brown edge corresponding to a dark terminal patch on the dorsal surface. Nape and neck above either black or grayish; in the former case the base of the ear behind is dark brown; in the latter it is white.

No. 252.—Body long and slender; limbs very long, ears very long, much longer than the head; tail of moderate length; legs slender, the fur compact and short; claws very long and sharp, nearly straight, projecting beyond the pads.

General color of the back a light brownish yellow, with a slight shade of cinnamon varied with black; somewhat similar on the sides, but paler, with less admixture of black. The nape is dark sooty brown. The upper chest and throat are dull brownish yellow; the sides of the rump and buttocks, the tibial region all round, and the outer surfaces of the fore legs, light ashy or bluish gray, finely and faintly marked with parallel lines of black, caused by the black tips of interspersed hairs. The tail is ashy white beneath and on the sides; black above, the color running up on the rump for two inches. Inferior surface of the body, anterior face of the hind feet, posterior edge of the fore legs, and the inferior surface of the head, white, with a tinge of smoky; most decided exteriorly and on the inside of the thighs; a whitish spot on the top of the head; the pads of the feet light dull brownish yellow. The internal and external bands of the ear are pale brownish yellow and black, finely mixed; the external fringe and the remaining portion of the outer surface of the ear, or its concavity, is unicolored brownish yellow, darker towards the top. The posterior edge is yellowish, or creamy white, except for about half an inch from the tip, which is dark brown. On the posterior surface or convexity the ear is sooty brown for half an inch from the tip (not on the external band) and at the base, the color extending on the posterior edge of the latter, or for nearly two inches. Of the remaining portion, the inferior half is pale fulvous, shading superiorly into ashy.

On the back the fur is light ash gray at the base, then black, then brownish yellow, and finally tipped with black. On the lower part of the sides the black changes into a light brown. On the posterior portion of the dorsal surface the bases of the hairs on the median region are lead color ; more laterally this becomes lighter, and the dorsal portion nearly white. The grey hairs on the buttocks are much shorter and more compressed than the adjacent region of the back.

A specimen, No. 135, collected at Eagle Pass, Texas, by Mr. Schott, in the summer of 1852, agrees in every respect, except in having the back of the neck entirely destitute of the dusky brown of the one first described. This is of a brownish yellow, the color showing on the base of the ear. The black annulation of the fur above is less extended and less intense. The ears are more cinnamon in tint, and the black at tip is a little greater in extent. The legs appear a little thicker and the pads fuller, the claws not quite so long and sharp ; the ears are no longer in proportion.

No. 134, likewise collected by Mr. Schott, at Eagle Pass, agrees with No. 252 in the dusky nape and the black base of the ears. The black on the back is, however, more like No. 135, or less distinct than in 252, and the fur on the anterior portion of the back is more dusky at the base. The claws are shorter, the pads rather fuller, and their color much darker, or a dirty reddish brown.

A specimen from Northern Mexico, Charco Escondido, collected in the spring of 1853 by Lt. Couch, U. S. A., bears a close resemblance to No. 252; but the ears are much longer in proportion, as will be seen from the table of measurements. The colors above are clearer, the brownish yellow lighter, the under surfaces of the feet darker ; the tail, too, is rather longer ; no other differences discernible. The nape and base of ears are dusky black.

A single pair of ears from Mr. Jennings, Austin, Texas, are larger than those of any specimen examined. I can detect no special difference from the others, except that the colors are purer, the black at the end of the ear covering an inch and a half from the tip, the inner surface, except the external band, pure white to the base.

Thus far, no specimens received in Washington seem to correspond to the *Lepus texanus* of Aud. and Bach. The characteristics of the specimens above described cover those of *L. texanus* to some extent. It will be seen that specimens with black napes have the ears varying by an inch, the largest nearly six inches. All have black tips to the ears, of greater or less extent, although authors give the black ends as peculiar to *L. californicus* and *texanus*. Specimens with the ears of the same proportional size have black napes or gray. The nearest approach to *L. texanus* is seen in a scalp with ears, brought from Red river by Capt. Marcy. Here the colors are more rufous than in any of the others; the nape is pale rusty ; the base of the ear white ; the tip brownish black, except on the external band. The ears measure 5 inches 2 lines posteriorly, and 4 inches 3 lines from the notch.

A young specimen, collected at Charco Escondido by Lt. Couch, has much the same distribution of color above as the adult. The fur, however, is fuller and brownish lead color at the roots, then brownish rusty, then black, then reddish yellow ; some of the hairs, in addition, have black tips ; towards the sides the base of the hairs becomes lighter. Upper part of tail and rump, black; abdomen, beneath, pure white, like cotton; beneath the head and anterior surface of hind feet grayish white; inner surface of the limbs ashy gray; the neck beneath rusty gray. Pads of the feet bright brownish red. Nape dusky, much as in the adult, but the colors less bright.

Total length, 11 inches; ears, two inches 2 lines, but little longer than the head; hind foot, 2 inches 9 lines.

Measurements.

	No. 252. Brazes, Tex. Black nape.	No. 135. Eagle Pass, Tex. Gray nape.	No. 134. Eagle Pass, Black nape.	No. 299. Chareo Escondido. Bl'k nape.	Llano Estacado. Gray nape.	Austin, Tex.
To base of ears	4.00	4.25	3.83	4.08	....	....
To base of tail	21.75	24.50	19.50	19.75	20.00	....
Tail to end of vertebrae	1.58	1.75	Broken.	2.25	2.25	....
Tail to end of hairs	2.75	2.83	Broken.	3.25	3.17	....
Ears posteriorly	5.17	5.42	4.83	5.83	5.25	6.25
Ears anteriorly	4.75	5.07	4.50	5.58	....	....
Ears above notch	4.00	4.58	4.25	4.93	4.75	5.00
Fore arm	5.00	....	4.17	....	....	....
Fore foot	2.25	2.93	2.17	2.17	....	....
Tibia	5.25	5.83	....	....	....	....
Hind foot	4.58	4.58	4.58	4.58	4.75	....

"The 'jackass rabbit,' so called because of its great ears, is the only mammal, excepting the wolf, that occurs abundantly on the naked prairies. It is easily put up, for it usually seeks no other protection or hiding place than a little scratch in the ground in the shade afforded by some stunted bush. Does not squat so readily as the *Lepus virginianus*, and never burrows for protection like *L. Artemisia*. In certain sections, during the winter, the coarse and stinking creosote plant constitute almost its only food. Its subsistence on such diet is evidence of its hardihood, and proves its capability of existence where most animals of its kind must perish. The traveller is at times glad to obtain it for food; yet its flesh is hard and dry, and sometimes highly, but not always pleasantly, flavored. Its great swiftness prevents it from falling an easy prey to wolves. I on one occasion saw this rabbit pursued by some large hawks; they seemed to be wary of their power to capture it, and did not attempt to seize it while in my sight. In plazas and other places, well beaten paths indicate the favorite haunt or play ground of this timid but watchful animal. When suddenly started up, especially if it is much frightened, its body is brought into a semi-circle, with ears laid close back, and its vigorous leaps are continued in one direction but a few hundred yards; it thus overcomes space under great disadvantages; its course, ordinarily even, is very zig-zag. If going at an easy jump its ears are thrown forward, reminding one of the flapping appendages of its prototype, jackass, unless endangered by the thorny vegetation; its prodigious leaps, which clear it of most of the flora in its habitat, however, save the trouble of any especial care in this respect. The contrast of color—black and white—about its tail and head is quite decided when running from you, the position in which it is usually seen. Its skin is as tender and it is as easily killed as other hares. It brings forth but two or three young at a time, and not till late in summer, so far as my observation went."—(J. H. Clark.)

57. LEPUS CALIFORNICUS, Gray (p. 594.)—California Hare.

One specimen of this species was collected on the lower Colorado river of California, by Mr. Schott.

58. LEPUS SYLVATICUS, Bachman (p. 597.)—Gray Rabbit.

A specimen, probably of this species, was collected at Indianola, Texas.

59. LEPUS ARTEMISIA, Bachman (p. 602.)—Sage Rabbit.

This species is abundant through Texas and New Mexico.

315. San Antonio to El Paso. J. H. Clark.—1417. Matamoras. Lt. D. N. Couch.

"Wherever the thorny clumps of chapparal and the loose sandy soil afford protection to this smallest of rabbits, it may be found in great numbers. No matter when or where one of these may be seen, a clump of chapparal or its burrow seem always at hand; thus it does not travel far, and a few jumps brings it to a place of safety. Notwithstanding this, it forms the principal animal food of the coyote. The burrows usually run into sand hillocks formed around bushes; sometimes, however, they are dug into the bare compact surface. Both this species and the *Callotis* seem to be lean in all localities, and under all circumstances, never having seen a specimen of either showing a deposit of fat around the kidney, so common on the *L. virginianus* in fall As an article of food it is superior to the *Callotis*, but not equal to the common hare; and on the lower Rio Grande, a region fertile in game, where it is particularly abundant, the people do not think it even worth the knocking over with a stick."—(J. H. Clark.)

60. LEPUS BACHMANI, Waterhouse (p. 606.)—Bachman's Hare.

Specimens of this species were collected at Brownsville, Texas, by Lt. Couch and Capt. Van Vliet.

61. DASYPUS NOVEM-CINCTUS, Linnaeus (p. 623.)—Texas Armadillo.

Sp. Ch.—Tail as long as the body, exclusive of the head. Shell of the back a little wider than long. Eight movable rings in the middle of the shell, and a ninth partly free on the sides. Tail covered with jointed whorls for its basal portion; the terminal third plated but not sheathed. Color blackish. Molars 32.

Description of a young specimen in alcohol.—The head is very much rounded at the vertex, but produced into a rather narrow truncated muzzle, the sides of which, viewed from above, are concave; the upper outline nearly straight from behind the eyes to the tip. The ears are broad, long, obtusely acuminate, and situated entirely on the occiput, their bases in contact. They are barely less than half the length of the head. The eyes are small; considerably nearer the occiput than the nose. The nostrils are entirely terminal, horizontally crescentic, the concavity superior; the broad truncated muzzle, with the nostrils separated by a rather wide septum, resembles very closely that of the hog.

The legs are very strong; the anterior projecting from the body quite as much as the posterior, and of equal thickness. On the fore feet there are four fingers without the slightest rudiment of a thumb; the toes very short; scarcely projecting in any of the feet beyond the thickened skin. The two central fore claws are much largest; the inner and outer much smaller and equal; the former more posterior, not reaching the base of the adjacent claw. The hind claws are rather shorter; the third longest; the second and fourth equal and opposite; the first and fifth also equal and opposite, and considerably further back. The tail is long, and tapers regularly to an acute tip; it is as long as the body, exclusive of the head.

The entire body is covered with tessellated bony plates; those on the back arranged in sheets, which come low down on the sides, but do not extend on to the belly. Of those there is one continuous sheet on the anterior third of the body, cut out so as to fit round the back of the head; the middle third is occupied by eight half rings, nearly equal to each other; and the posterior third is again covered by a sheet of plates extending to the tail, and fitting down over the rump and thighs. The connexions between these sheets and rings are formed by a skin covered with minute tessellations, and permitting free motion. In addition to the eight rings described, there is a slight indication of a ninth posterior one, which, however, only becomes free and open on the lower part of the sides. The tail is enveloped in whorls of plates, of which twelve may be counted from the base, each one composed of two or three single whorls or annuli between successive joints, the posterior one with the plates more elongated; after this the plates become imbricated, as in a plaited whip lash, without special joints. The plates on the top of the head are sub-hexagonal, and of nearly equal size. Those on the shoulders and rump are rounded, and chiefly arranged so that one larger plate is surrounded entirely by smaller ones; the plates on the rings are narrowly elongated triangular, the apices and bases of the triangles alternating.

As stated, the entire exterior of the animal is covered with plates; those on the ear smallest; the under and inner surfaces are covered with granulations, arranged in transverse series. A good many short stiff scattered hairs are seen to project from the under surface, as well as from the edges of the sheets and annuli above.

In five specimens before me from Texas, three very young and two adult, there is a very great constancy in the arrangement of the rings on the middle of the body; of these, eight separated narrow ones are visible on the middle of the back, and nine when counted on the side. In a shell from Brazil, (2,195,) the breadth is greater in proportion, and there are nine separated annuli above. The sculpturing also is slightly different. It is not at all impossible that a careful comparison of perfect specimens from Texas and South America may reveal specific differences.

The skull has eight molars in each side of each jaw, or thirty-two in all.

The nine banded armadillo has thus far been found to occur in the territory of the United States only on the Lower Rio Grande, although extending southward through Mexico, and if identical with South American specimens, into Brazil and Paraguay.

2859. Matamoras, Mexico. Lieut. Couch.—230. Lower Rio Grande, Texas. J. H. Clark.

"The inhabitants of the former Spanish colonies know the tatou commonly as the *Armadillo* or *Encubierto*. The people of the country esteem its flesh; and the women attribute imaginary properties to its shell. This animal is mostly nocturnal in its habits, rarely going out by day, near the settlements, except to search for food. It delights to dig large holes in the earth, where it conceals flesh and vegetable substances. A viscous and transparent humor almost continually drops from its mouth. This edentate is naturally stupid. It is gifted with extraordinary strength, and when it has once taken hold in its burrow, it is more easily torn to pieces than pulled out.

"I have sometimes seen these animals elevate a weight placed on their backs of almost a hundred pounds.

"As the movements of this animal are very awkward, it seldom escapes the hunter who pursues it on the open plain; but in the mountains it rolls itself up, and thus transformed into a ball, on a declivity rapidly disappears, rolling over the stones.

"A specimen of which I made a description was kept two or three months in our house. It frequented the kitchen, where it lived on the refuse; and if it came out sometimes in the day from its den, which it had dug in the earth, it was not long before it returned again to it.

"At will this animal can entirely conceal its head between its legs, as when it sleeps or when it is attacked."—(Berlandier)

"The occurrence of this animal any distance east of the Rio Grande is probably unknown, nor is it found higher up on this river than the vicinity of Ringgold Barracks. It lives mostly in and about the banks of the river and the many lakes or old river beds. It sleeps, for the most part, during the day, so drawing itself up that all of the few vulnerable parts are completely protected by its armor. Among the inhabitants it is much sought after as food, and is considered a delicate dish. Its flavor is similar to that of the "possum;" but less fat, more delicate, and altogether more palatable. It is inoffensive, has a gentle disposition, and can be handled with impunity. Once in the hands of its captor, it will play possum, allowing itself to be carried leisurely by the tail, so that an unexpected and spasmodic jerk, such as it only is capable of giving, will release it from the most vigorous grasp, particularly if there is any support for its feet. So rapid and vigorous are the movements of its powerful claws, that but a few minutes are necessary for the animal to melt away from your view in the most compact soil."—(J. H. Clark.)

62. DICOTYLE TORQUATUS, Cuv. (p. 627.) Texas Peccary.

This species was occasionally met with by the Commission along the Rio Grande, but under circumstances when it was not convenient to preserve any skins.

"This annimal habitually lives in the bottom lands of the water courses; it is not confined to such places, as it is not unfrequently seen on the prairie singly, or in a drove. Many stories are told of its ferocity; of its attacks without provocation; no manifest evidence of such a disposition came under my observation, though I have seen it chased and wounded repeatedly. In open ground it is somewhat shy, and for a hog runs with fleetness; and when pursued will dodge and squat with at least as much facility and success as a jack-ass rabbit. Its vicinity is easily detected by an odor, which, though less intense, is not much less offensive than that of the skunk. There is a swamp near Ringgold Barracks that perfumes the whole neighborhood with the odor of the peccary, and is known as the "wild-hog den," by which name (wild-hog) it goes among frontier men. The Mexicans apply to it the same term (moran) that they do to the domestic hog. Live Oak creek, a rivulet emptying into the Pecos near its lower crossing, is noted for the great number of peccaries inhabiting its course.

"The food of the peccary in southwestern Texas consists mainly of acorns and pecans; further west, and in higher regions, these sources of subsistence fail, and the occurrence of the animal is consequently rarer. The absence of any largely developed posterior appendage, usually designated as the tail, is the most characteristic and striking feature, not excepting the secretory sac, resting skin deep only on the rump, and which emits the odor. Neither the immediate removal of this sac, nor any other precaution or process, could render its lean and stringy hams palatable. Like the domestic hog, it both wallows and roots; the meagre traces in these respects show that the wild hog is less industrious than its domestic representative."—(J. H. Clark.)

"The peccary is not an uncommon animal in southwestern Texas. It is met with in greater or less numbers along all of the streams, and is especially numerous along Devil's river, Live Oak creek and the Pecos river. West of the Rio Grande we observed them only at San Bernardino.

"They are almost always associated in herds, composed of from five to ten individuals, and are very rarely found alone. They prefer the thickest and most impenetrable bushes, from which they are not easily driven out. In the localities where they are very numerous, their proximity, especially after sunset, may be discovered by the peculiar order which they emit, and which is not entirely unlike that of the skunk, (*Mephitis*,) though of less intensity; this we particularly observed in travelling up the Pecos river.

"They sometimes become quite vicious, and might prove a dangerous antagonist on account of their sharp tusks and great activity.

"If one of a herd is wounded, the remainder will often turn and attack the assailant with great fierceness and desperation.

"In their choice of food they seem to give preference to pecans, walnuts, and acorns, though they also eat roots and other substances."—(Dr. Kennerly.)

63. CERVUS VIRGINIANUS, Boddaert, (p. 643.) Virginia Deer.

This species is abundant in many parts of Texas, though no specimens were collected.

"On the prairies near the coast this animal supplants the antelope and the black-tailed deer. It may be seen here grazing among the cattle of the settlements, where it is wilder and more difficult of approach than in wholly unfrequented regions. On the plains of northwest Texas and further westward the occurrence of the common deer is somewhat rare, and principally confined to the water-courses, where, besides the water and grass, is the additional attraction of trees and bushes, which serve as protection from the northers in winter and from the heat of the sun in summer. In the country lying between the Nueces and the Rio Grande, more deer were seen in one day than a week's travel disclosed in any other region traversed by the Boundary Commission. It is less gregarious than the antelope, but more so than the black-tailed deer; this latter prefers mountainous regions, and is never seen in company with the red deer."—(J. H. Clark.)

64. CERVUS MEXICANUS, Gmelin, (p. 653.) Sonora Deer.

"The Virginian deer, so common throughout the entire State of Texas, and particularly its southwestern portion, was also observed by us in considerable numbers in various localities west of the Rio Grande. Indeed, we believe that few species of animals are so generally spread over the entire continent as this, and at the same time in such great numbers. It was observed in the valleys of all the streams passed by us in our journey from El Paso to Los Nogales, as well as in the various mountain ranges, particularly the San Luis and Sierra Madre. In the valley of the Santa Cruz river and the adjacent country we found them in such numbers as to influence the belief that a few skilful hunters might have supplied our entire party with fresh meat.

The Mexicans of this region, having but few fire-arms, and boing very much afraid of the Indians, do not often hunt them. Indeed, thirty miles west of the village of Santa Cruz, these animals seemed to be so unaccustomed to the sound of a gun that we have known them, when the hunter was concealed, to be fired at several times before becoming sufficiently alarmed to take flight.

"During our stay at Los Nogales in the month of June, particularly the latter part, the heat during the day was quite oppressive; and the valleys of the streams, with their thick undergrowth affording a good protection from the rays of the sun, were the favorate places of resort for these animals. Very early in the morning they were found feeding on the hills, but retired under the shelter of the bushes about ten o'clock, after which time they could be killed as easily as rabbits, by the hunter passing through the undergrowth with a gun charged with buck-shot. They would rarely spring from their concealment until approached within twenty paces.

"At this season, June, the horns of the bucks were but a few inches in length, and the females generally far advanced in pregnancy. We observed often the young of the previous year still following the doe, which was about to bring forth another progeny."—(Dr. Kennerly.)

65. CERVUS MACROTIS, Say, (p. 656.) Black tailed Deer.

"We did not observe this animal until we reached the vicinity of the valley of the Corralitos river, and here it was not very common. It was rarely seen in the immediate valley of the river, except late in the afternoon, just before sunset, when it came to drink, but preferred the neighboring mountains or hills. In the San Luis mountains and the Sierra Madre they were very numerous; but we noticed, while near these localities, that this species is much more apt to be driven from its accustomed haunts than the other, (*Cervus virginianus.*) In a few weeks, although at first equally as numerous, if not more so, than the latter, it disappeared almost entirely, while the red deer became only a little more shy, but its numbers did not seem to diminish.

"It is somewhat curious that we did not observe the black-tailed deer after leaving the Sierra Madre, although it is found in great numbers in California. The belt of country traversed by us, included between that mountain and the 111th meridian, seemed to be almost, if not entirely, without this animal, while in several localities the Virginian deer and antelope were both very common."—(Dr. Kennerly.)

66. ANTILOCAPRA AMERICANA, Ord. (p. 665.) Prong Horn Antelope; Cabree.

This species is abundant in Texas, although no skins were collected by the survey.

"On the plains lying between the Nueces and the Rio Grande, the great mustang range, and where the common deer is very abundant, but few antelopes are to be seen. It is not till west of the Pecos is reached that droves are observed dotting the most open and naked prairies, which it undoubtedly prefers and habitually inhabits; it is no rare occurrence, however, to find it in mountain valleys, from which it will sometimes take to the mountains, but usually from fright, not choice. Being shy, and quick to take alarm, it always keeps at a great distance. Occasionally one, either dumfounded with fear or overcome with curiosity, will come right up to a train by a series of advances and reconnaissances, while the rest of the herd are lost to the sight in an opposite direction. It is on plains destitute of most forms of vegetation except grass that the largest herds of this animal are to be found. When it is considered that such prairies cover an extent of fifty or even one hundred miles in some directions without water, its adaptability to the regions inhabited is manifest. There is no bond of sympathy between the antelope and the deer, for they are never seen herding together, and seldom occupying common ground. The absence of water and luxuriant grass in the antelope region may account in a measure for the rarity of the deer. Though much scattered when feeding quietly, a herd flocks together as it runs off. The most remarkable habit of the antelope is its tendency to take and continue but one direction in its flight; so determined and obstinate is its disposition in this respect as to be impelled across arroyos, over mountains, and even through trains. To start it as a common deer is an unheard of thing, due to watchfulness rendered easy by the openness of the country inhabited. Shades of color varying from a deep fawn to an almost pure white are observable at a distant view in the same herd Its motion is more rapid as well as more regular than that of the deer, never leaping like the latter animal. Its flesh is also juicier and finer; its superiority is appreciable even by one who can make no pretension to an epicurean taste. Frontier men have assured me that they have sabred the antelope on ordinary horses during sleety weather, when they say it is unable to keep its feet. The wonderment that this animal sometimes expresses, and its apparent inability to see things aright, leads to the suggestion of some peculiarity in the eye, either of construction or position; its location on the side of the face, and directly at the base of the horn, would impress any one with its singularity. An allusion to its preference for open prairies as a habitat has already been made. This region, it will be remembered, is the home of the prairie dog, and its dependents, the rattlesnake, the owl, and the Holbrookia. The antelope is said to have an abiding hatred for the rattlesnake, which it decoys first into a striking attitude, and then utterly annihilates by leaping into the air and coming down upon it with its four sharp-cutting hoofs placed together."—(J. H. Clark.)

"On several occasions we have travelled over the road between San Antonio, Texas, and El Paso, on the Rio Grande, but we never have observed the antelope in that country until after crossing the Pecos river, and from that stream as far as the Rio Grande found it always the most common of the larger species of quadrupeds. On the immense plains and wide valleys stretching out from the Limpia mountains in all directions large herds are often seen. The number of individuals composing a herd vary from eight or ten to several hundred. We have often seen more than a hundred together, and perhaps sometimes as many as three hundred.

"In going westward from the Rio Grande we found them equally as numerous as in the country east of that stream, as far as we travelled. In the northern part of Sonora they were very common, and for the most part less shy and more easily captured than in other localities. In the less frequented regions the hunter has only partially to conceal himself and shake his hat or handkerchief, thus attracting the attention of the animals, whose curiosity is so great as to cause them to approach within gun-shot. This approach, however, is not made without apparent caution, for while performing it they walk very slowly, often stopping, and should they get to the windward of the hunter beat a rapid retreat, and soon disappear in the distance.

"In the northern part of the States of Chihuahua and Sonora we found the females very far advanced in pregnancy about the middle of July."—(Dr. Kennerly.)

OVIS MONTANA, (p. 673.) Big Horn; Mountain Sheep.

Of this animal no specimens were collected, though frequently seen by the Commission.

"*The Mountain Sheep, Big Horn, of the Americans of California and New Mexico; Borrego cimaron, of the Sonorians; Tenatzali, of the Apaches; Tajé, of the Cochimés of Lower California.*—The rocky sierras of northwestern Sonora, where want of water not only forbids the existence of every other species of ruminant, and where even the coyote, with all his cunning and tenacity, is nearly ruled out, are the favorite home of the mountain sheep.

"The state of drainage peculiar to a country seems to establish principally the existence of one or the other species of those ruminants, which are indigenous to the regions adjacent to the boundary line.

"Thus, the common deer belongs to the more shady lowlands, the mule deer to the uplands; the antelope ranges over the open mountain table lands, whilst the mountain sheep has its home over the rugged crests of the waterless sierras of north-western Sonora and New Mexico.

"Whilst surveying along the boundary line, I had sometimes occasion to leisurely observe these shy and comparatively rare animals upon their native ground. As usually an unarmed man is always led nearest to game, so was I on one day, walking almost side by side at eight to ten yards distance, with a large ram, which certainly stood upon his legs nearly four feet high above ground, with a length of five feet from head to tail.

"One whole afternoon, (I was waiting then for signals from another station,) a singular noise in the cliffs of an opposite mountain slope fixed my attention, and it was some hours before I was able to find out the real nature of it. It sounded as if a rock had been precipitated somewhere, and I first inclined to be satisfied with that; but as the sound, after certain intervals, was so often repeated, and the game lasted until evening, I attributed it to something else, until I seized upon the correct idea. The noise was nothing else than the result of a butting combat between two rams. On the whole of these mountain tops there was not a single horizontal or gently inclined spot where the round footprints of this animal could not be observed. In some places well beaten pathways lead up to the most rugged portions of the rocky sierras, where man hardly may trust his foot, lest he may be precipitated with the loosened detritus of weather-washed decomposed rocks. The water on which the inhabitants of these forsaken desert mountains depend are mostly but rain-water holes, (tinajas,) in which, during the hot season, water must become scarce enough.

"I have been assured by hunters that a flock or drove of these big horns, when closely pursued, will not shrink from a general leap over a precipice of one hundred and more feet deep to effect their escape. It is also stated that they do so without any risk, but escape, every one uninjured, by throwing themselves head foremost upon the heaviest portion of their gigantic horns, the spiral shape of which seems to paralyze the hardest shock. This, if not a fact, is at least generally believed. It is also not a modern invention, for Clavigero mentions the same, as he heard it from the lips of the California Indians.

"The horns of the mountain sheep are most formidable weapons for defence even against larger enemies; as, for instance, wolf or puma. The nature of the ground where the mountain sheep ranges hardly permits any ambush on the part of the aggressor, because there is no timber or brushwood. To meet a blow of those gigantic horns must be rather a risk of life; the more so, when an attacked big horn succeeds in driving his antagonist between a rocky wall and his 'battering ram.'"—(A. Schott.)

67. BOS AMERICANUS, Gmelin. (p. 682.) American Buffalo.

No skins of this species were collected by the Boundary Commission, though skulls and skeletons were frequently met with.

ALPHABETICAL INDEX.

EXPLANATION OF THE PLATES.

PLATE I.

Fig. 1—*Vespertilio pallidus*, Lec.—1045.—San Elizario, Texas.
1. *a*—side view of the head.

Fig. 2—*Macrotus californicus*, Baird.—Fort Yuma.
2. *a*—side view of the head; 2. *b*—back view of do., showing the membrane connecting the ears.

PLATE II.

Fig. 1—*Felis eyra*, Desm.—Matamoras.—Reduced from a drawing by Dr. Berlandier.

Fig. 2—*Putorius frenatus*, Aud. Bach.—Matamoras.—Young animal, before shedding its milk teeth. From an alcoholic specimen.
2. *a*—side view of the head; 2. *b*—roof of the mouth, showing the ridges of the palate; 2. *c*—under view of the fore foot; 2. *d*—under view of the hind foot, showing the naked turbercles.

PLATE III.

Fig. 1—*Didelphys californica*, Bennett.—Fig. 1, adult, No. 138.—Fig. 2, young, No. 199.

PLATE IV.

Sciurus limitis, Baird.—Devil's river, Texas.

PLATE V.

Sciurus castanonotus, Baird.—Copper Mines.

PLATE VI.

Fig. 1—*Tamias dorsalis*, Baird.—Copper Mines.
1. *a*—hairs of the tail separate, to show the annulation.

Fig. 2—*Sigmodon berlandieri*, Baird.—Adult.—Rio Nasas, Coahuila, Mexico.

PLATE VII.

Spermophilus grammurus, Bach.—(perhaps *S. macrurus.*)—Details from a specimen in alcohol, No. 1046.—Los Nogales.

1. *a*—view of head from the front; 1. *b*—do. from the side; 1. *c*—do. from beneath; 1. *d*—under view of fore foot; 1. *e*—do. of hind foot.

Fig. 2—*Spermophilus tereticauda*, Baird.—No. 1584.—Fort Yuma.

2. *a*—head from the side; 2. *b*—do. from before; 2. *c*—under view of fore foot; 2. *d*—do. of hind foot.

Fig. 3—*Spermophilus spilosoma*, Bennett.—No. 1042.—Janos.

3. *a*—head from the side; 3. *b*—do. from before; 3. *c*—do. from beneath; 3. *d*—under view of fore foot; 3. *e*—do. of hind foot.

Fig. 4—*Reithrodon.*—Janos to San Luis Spring, New Mexico.

4. *a*—ear; 4. *b*—under surface of fore foot; 4. *c*—do. of hind foot; the last two magnified three diameters.

PLATE VIII.

Thomomys umbrinus, Baird.—No. 154.—Copper Mines.

a—under surface of left fore foot; *b*—its longest claw from the side; *c*—do. from below; *d*—under surface of hind foot.

PLATE IX.

Fig. 1—*Geomys clarkii*, Baird.—No. 6.—Presidio del Norte.

1. *a*—under surface of left fore foot; 1. *b*—side view of its longest claw; 1. *c*—under view of do.; 1. *d*—under surface of left hind foot.

Fig. 2—*Perognathus hispidus*, Baird.—No. 577.. Charco Escondido, Mex.—From alcohol.

Fig. 3—*Dipodomys ordii*, Woodhouse.—Coahuila.—From alcohol.

PLATE X.

Fig. 1—*Thomomys umbrinus* Baird?—No. 1036.—Espia.

1. *a*—side view of head; 1. *b*—under view of do., showing the openings of the pouches; 1. *c*—under surface of the fore foot, (the metacarpal portion much foreshortened;) 1. *d*—do. hind foot.

Fig. 2—*Sigmodon berlandieri*, Baird.—No. 1034.—Los Nogales.

2. *a*—side view of head, showing the ear; 2. *b*—under view of the muzzle; 2. *c*—under view of the left fore foot; 2. *d*—side view of its longest claw; 2. *e*—under view of left hind foot; *f*—side view of the longest claw.

N. B. The engraver has neglected to represent the hairs under the nostrils.

Fig. 3—*Neotoma mexicana*, Baird.—No. 1033.—San Pedro, Sonora.

3. *a*—side view of the head; 3. *b*—muzzle from beneath; 3. *c*—under surface of left fore foot; 3. *d*—its longest toe and claw; 3. *e*—under surface of hind foot; 3. *f*—its longest toe and claw.

Fig. 4—*Perognathus flavus*, Baird.—No. 1043.—San Antonio to El Paso.

4. *a*—side view of head; 4. *b*—under view of do., showing the cheek pouches; 4. *c*—under view of left fore foot; 4. *d*—do. of hind foot; (the feet magnified three times.)

Fig. 5—*Perognathus flavus*, Baird.—No. 1041.—Los Nogales.

The references the same as in fig. 4; the feet also magnified three diameters.

NOTE.—In this figure the posterior plantar tubercle has been omitted by the engraver; as also the furrows in the anterior faces of the upper incisors, both here and in figure 4.

Fig. 6—*Reithrodon* ——— ?—No. 1039.—Janos to San Luis Spring.

6. *a*—side of head; 6. *b*—under surface of left fore foot; 6. *c*—do. of left hind foot. The feet magnified three diameters.

PLATE XI.

Fig. 1—*Felis concolor*, Linn.—No. 1148.—Eagle Pass, Texas.—Adult; about two-thirds the natural size.

a—skull from below; *b*—do. from above; *c*—do. from the side; *d*—left side of lower jaw; *e*—do. from above.

Fig 2—*Felis concolor*—No. 1110.—Copper Mines.—Young, still having the milk teeth; skull natural size.

a—side view of left upper teeth; *b*—right upper teeth from below; *c*—left side of lower jaw.

PLATE XII.

Felis pardalis, Linn.—No. 1359.—Matamoras, Mex.—Adult; skull natural size. References *a–e*, as in Plate XI, fig. 1.

PLATE XIII.

Fig. 1—*Felis pardalis*, Linn.—No. 1360.—Matamoras.—Young, with temporary teeth; skull natural size. References *a–e*, as in fig. 1, Plate XI.

Fig. 2—*Felis eyra*, Desm.—No. 1373.—Matamoras, Mex.—Adult; skull natural size. References *a–e*, as in the last.

PLATE XIV.

Fig. 1—*Felis yaguarundi*, Desm.—No. 1426.—Matamoras.—Adult; skull natural size. References *a–e*, as usual.

Fig. 2—*Bassaris astuta*, Licht.—No. 1619.—El Paso, Texas.—Adult female; skull natural size. References *a–e*, as usual.

PLATE XV.

Fig. 1—*Lynx maculatus?*—No. 1370.—Matamoras.—Quite young, with the permanent teeth, however; skull natural size. References *a–e*.

Fig. 2—*Lynx maculatus?*—No. 1371.—Matamoras.—Skull, with the temporary teeth, natural size. References *a–e*.

PLATE XVI.

Canis latrans, Say.—No. 999.—Copper Mines, New Mexico.—Skull reduced to about two-thirds natural size. References *a–e*.

PLATE XVII.

Fig. 1—*Putorius frenatus*, Aud. & Bach.—No. 1172.—Lower Rio Grande.—Skull of adult, natural size. References *a–e*.

Fig. 2—*Putorius frenatus*, Aud. & Bach.—No. 1725.—Matamoras.—Skull of young, with the temporary teeth; natural size. References *a–e*.

Fig. 3—*Mephitis bicolor*, Gray.—No. 1621.—Indianola, Texas.—Adult; skull natural size. References *a–e*.

PLATE XVIII.

Procyon hernandezii, Wiegm.—No. 1386.—Matamoras, Mexico.—Adult; skull natural size. References *a–e*.

PLATE XIX.

Ursus cinnamomeus?—No. 992.—Copper Mines.—Adult skull. Reduced to less than two-thirds. References *a–e*.

PLATE XX.

Ursus horribilis, var. *horreaeus*, Baird.—No. 995.—Copper Mines.—Young skull, with the permanent teeth; *a–e*, as in the preceding plates; all reduced to one-third the natural size; *f*—left upper teeth from the outside; *g*—do. from below; *h*—left lower from the outside; *i*—do. from above; *f–i*, natural size.

PLATE XXI.

Fig. 1—*Sciurus limitis*, Baird.—No. 1265.—Devil's river, Texas.—Skull natural size. References *a—e*.

Fig. 2—*Sciurus castanonotus*, Baird.—No. 1107.—Copper Mines, New Mexico.—Skull natural size. References *a–e*.

Fig. 3—*Spermophilus couchii*, Baird.—No. 1255.—Santa Catarina, Mexico.—Skull. References *a–e*, natural size; *f*—left upper molars from below; *g*—left lower molar from above; *f* and *g* about one-half greater than natural size.

Fig. 4—*Spermophilus tereticauda*, Baird.—No. 2419.—Fort Yuma, Cal.—Skull. References as in preceding figure, (*a–g*,) *f* and *g* nearly twice natural size.

PLATE XXII.

Fig. 1—*Spermophilus grammurus*, Bach.—No. 1111.—Copper Mines, New Mexico.—Skull natural size. References *a–e*.

Fig. 2—*Spermophilus mexicanus*, Licht.—No. 1267.—Brownsville, Texas.—Skull natural size. References *a–e*.

Fig. 3—*Spermophilus spilosoma*, Bennet.—No. 1323.—El Paso.—Skull.—*a–e*, natural size; *f*—left upper molars from below; *g*—left lower molars from above; *f–g*, rather more than twice natural size.

PLATE XXIII.

Fig. 1—*Geomys clarkii*, Baird.—No. 1624.—Presido del Norte. Skull.—*a–e*, natural size; *f*—left upper molars from below; *g*—left lower molars from above; *f–g* magnified nearly three times.

Fig. 2—*Dipodomys agilis*, Gambel.—No. 1630.—Monterey, Cal.—Skull. *a–e*, natural size; *f*—left upper molars from below; *g*—left lower molars from above; *h*—front view of upper incisors; *f–h*, magnified a little more than twice.

Fig. 3—*Dipodomys ordii*, Woodhouse.—No. 1632.—Western Texas.—Skull. References *a–h*, as in the last figure.

Fig. 4—*Dipodomys ordii*, var. *montanus*.—No. 1631.—Upper Rio Grande valley. *a*—left upper molars from below; *b*—left lower molars from above; *c*—front view of upper incisors. Magnified about twice.

Fig. 5—*Thomomys umbrinus*, Baird.—No. 1231.—Sonora.—Skull. References *a–g* as in fig. 1; *f* and *g* magnified nearly three times.

Fig. 6—*Perognathus hispidus*, Baird.—No. 1696.—Female.—Charco Escondido, Mexico.—Skull. References *a–g*, as in fig. 1; *f–g* magnified rather more than twice.

PLATE XXIV.

Fig. 1—*Neotoma mexicana*, Baird.—No. 260.—Colorado bottom.—Skull. *a*—from below; *b*—from above; *c*—from the side; *d*—left side of lower jaw; *e*—do. from above; all of natural size; *f*—left upper molars from below; *g*—left lower molars from above; *f* and *g* magnified nearly three times.

Fig. 2—*Neotoma micropus*, Baird.—No. 1676.—Male.—Charco Escondido, Mexico.—Skull. References *a–g*, as in the preceding figure; *f* and *g* magnified nearly three times.

Fig. 3—*Sigmodon berlandieri*, Baird.—No. 1667.—Coahuila, Mexico.—Skull. References *a–g*, as in figure 1; *f* and *g* magnified nearly three times.

Fig. 4—*Reithrodon megalotis*, Baird.—No. 2281.—Janos to San Luis Spring, New Mexico.—Skull. References *a–g*, as in fig. 1; *f–g* magnified nearly three times.

PLATE XXV.

Fig. 1—*Lepus callotis*, var. *flavogularis*?—No. 1215.—San Antonio to El Paso.—Skull natural size. References *a–e*.

Fig. 2—*Lepus artemisia*, Bach.—No. 1232.—San Antonio to El Paso.—Skull natural size. References *a–e*.

PLATE XXVI.

Dasypus novemcinctus, Linn.—No. 1409—Matamoras, Mexico.—Skull natural size. References *a–e*.

PLATE XXVII.

Fig. 1—*Dicotyles torquatus*, Cuv.—No. 1101.—Female.—Brownsville, Texas.—Skull; teeth partly worn. References *a–e*, half natural size; *f*—right upper molars from the side; *g*—left upper molar from below; *h*—left lower molar from the side; *i*—do. from above; *f–i* natural size.

Fig. 2—*Dicotyles torquatus*, Cuv.—No. 1008.—Rio Grande.—Teeth as of a younger animal, with the crowns unworn; *a*—left upper molars from the side; *b*—do. from below; *c*—left lower molars from the side; *d*—do. from above. All natural size.

H. Richard del. R. Metzeroth sc.

Fig. 1.

Richard del. R. Metzeroth sc.

F. Metzeroth fec.

H. Richard del. R. Metzeroth sc.

Richard del. T. Metzeroth sc.

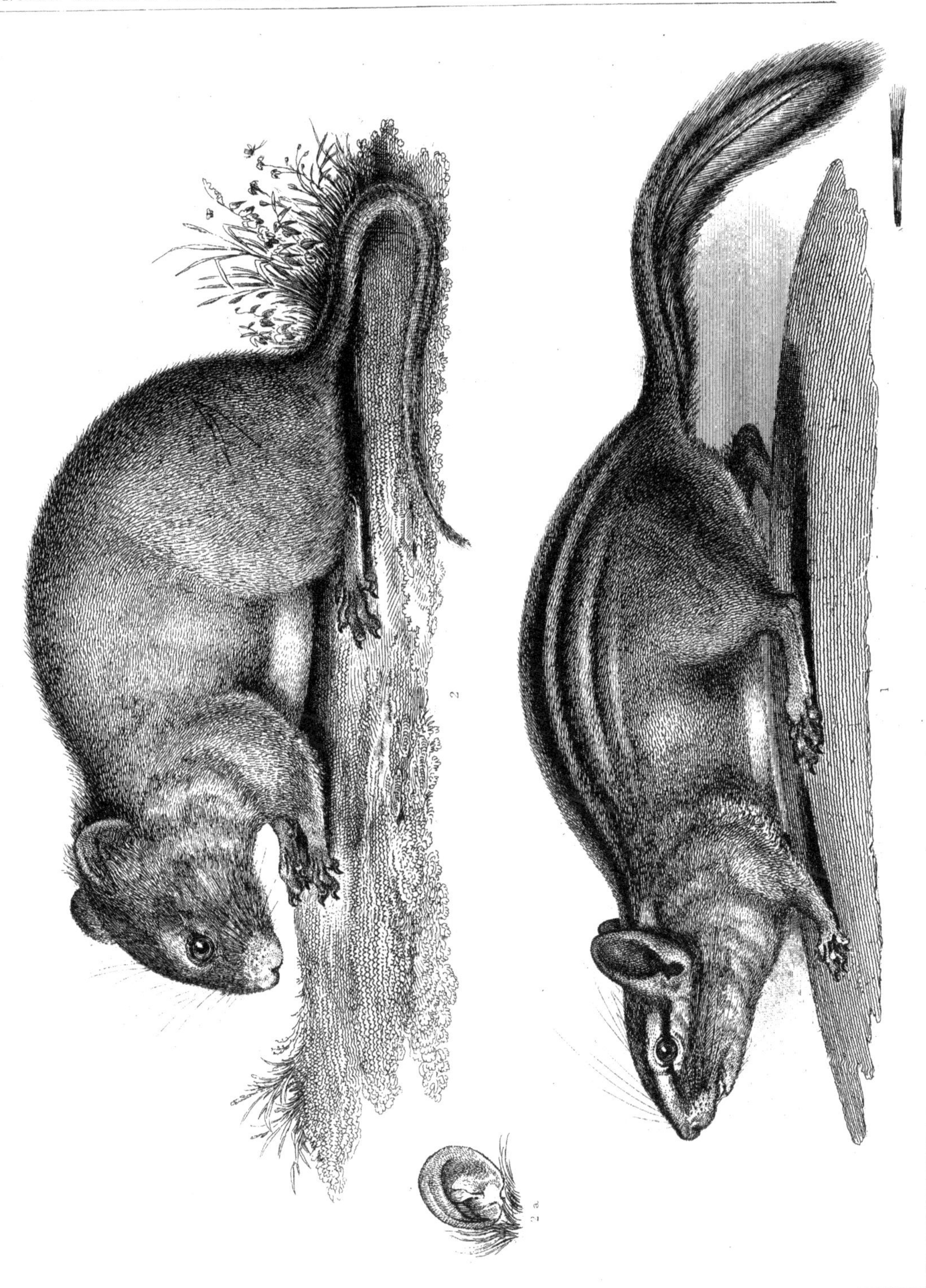

J.H. Richard del. R. Metzerott sc.

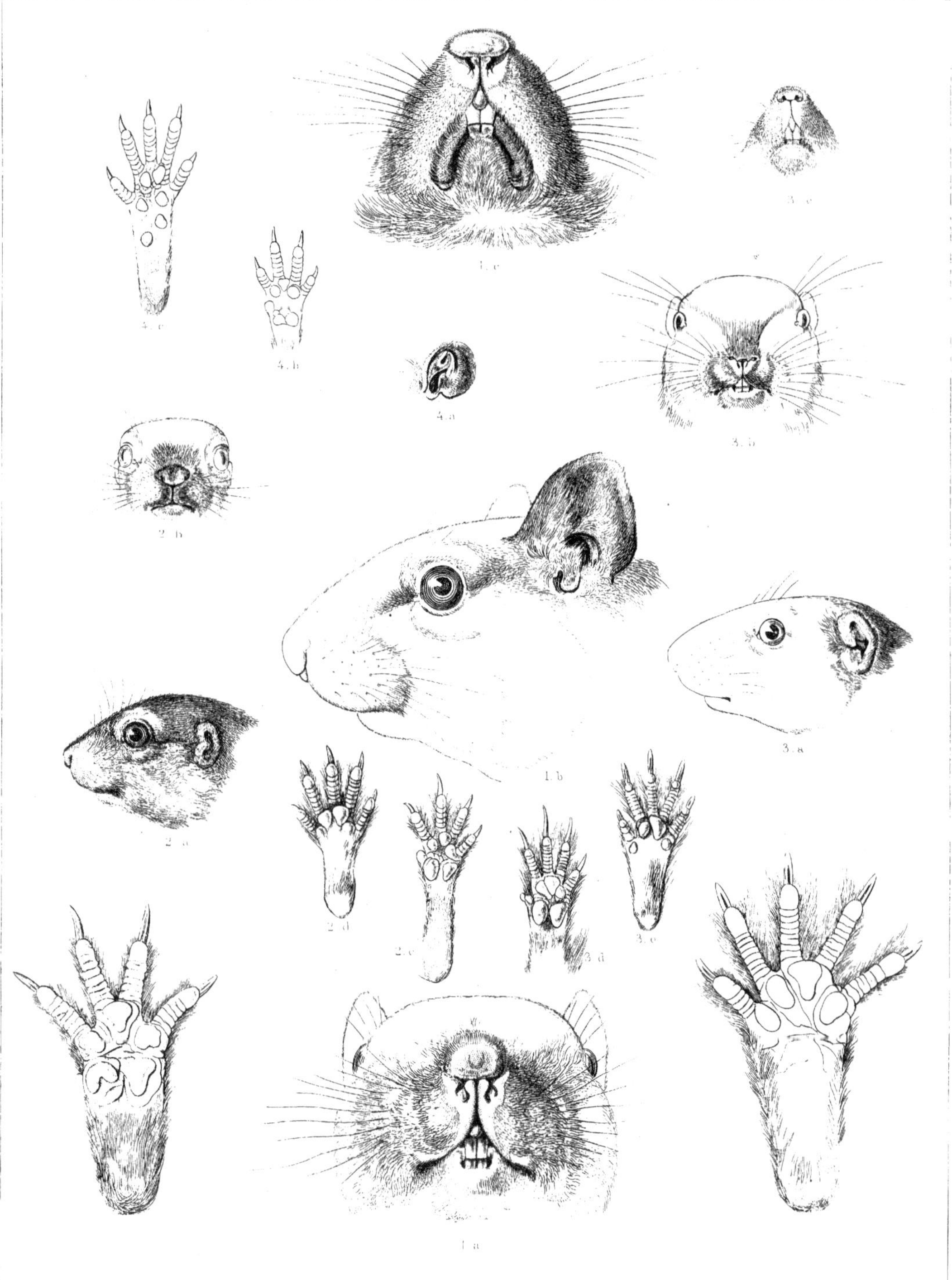

J.H. Richard del.

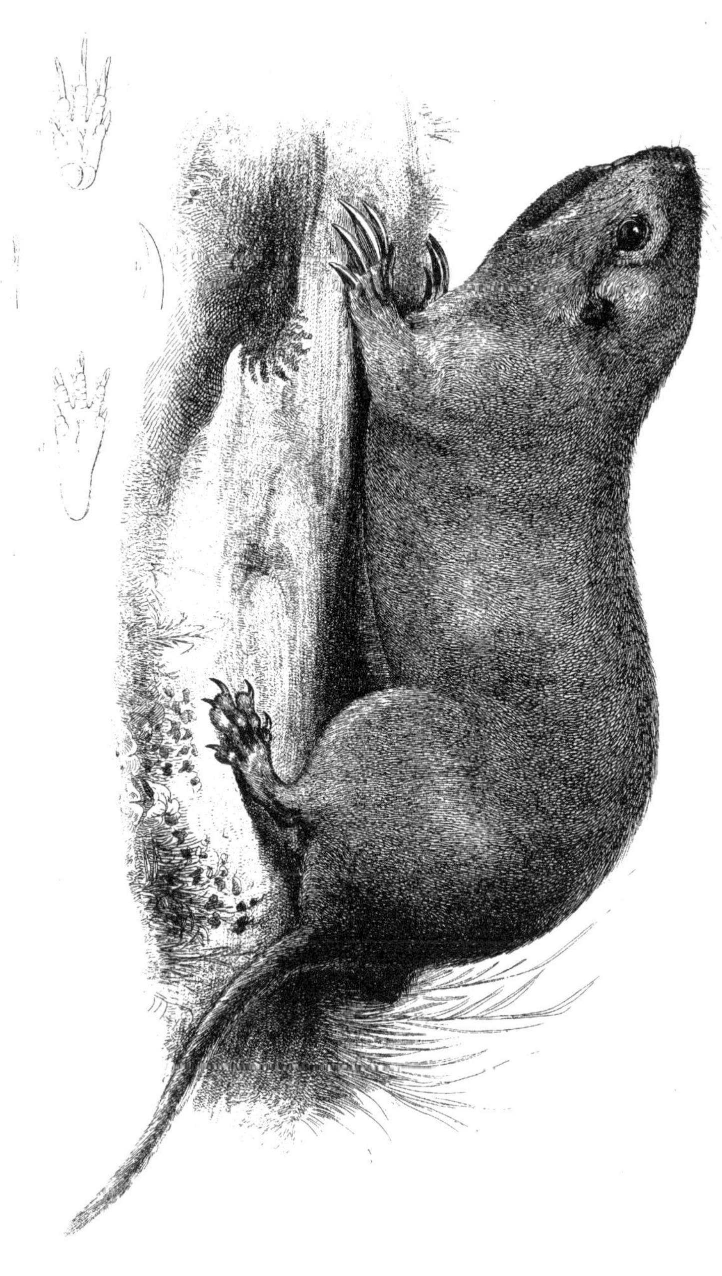

chant del. R. Metzeroth sc.

H. Richard del.

R. Metzerott sc.

R. Metzeroth sc.

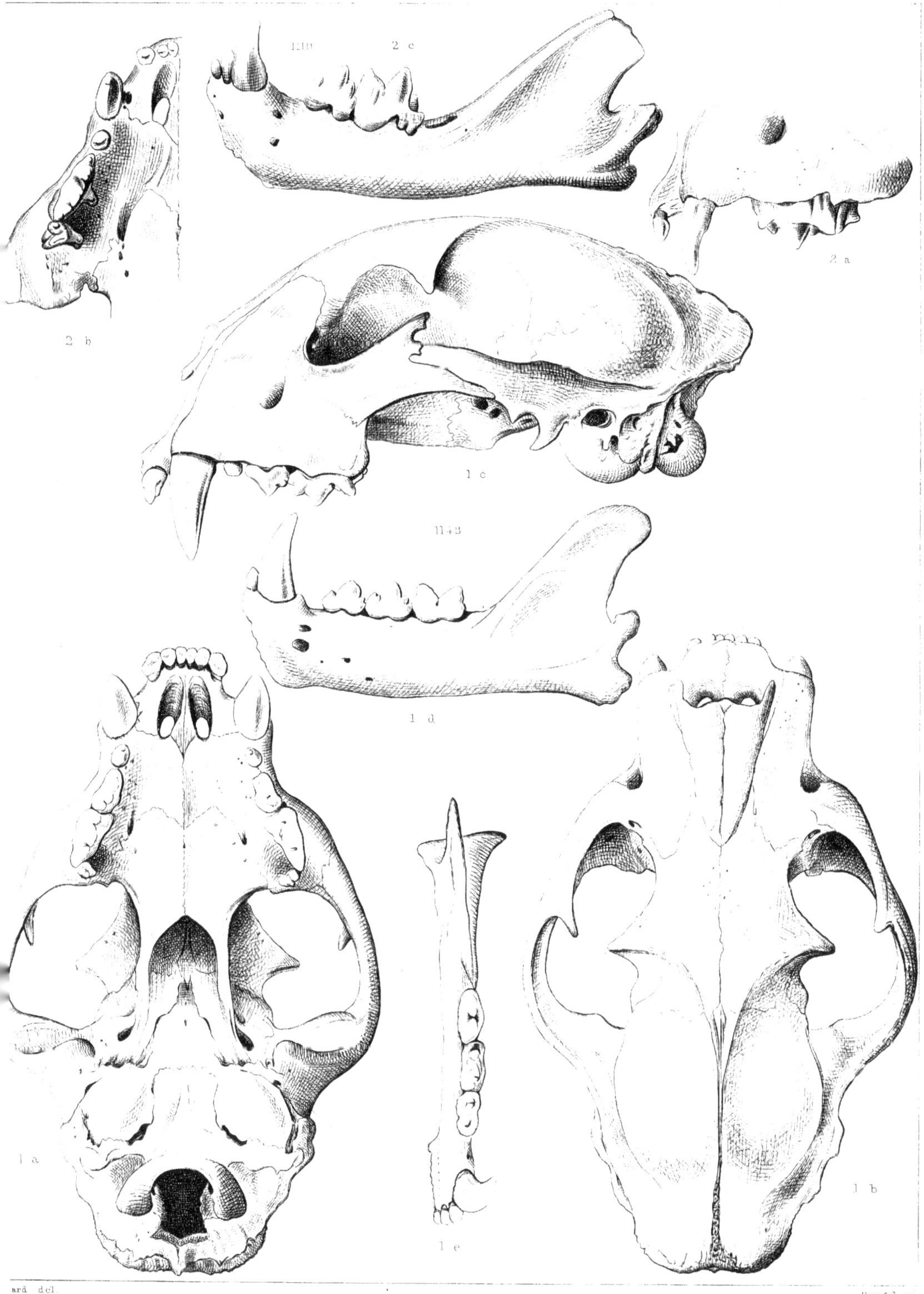

ard del. Dougal sc.

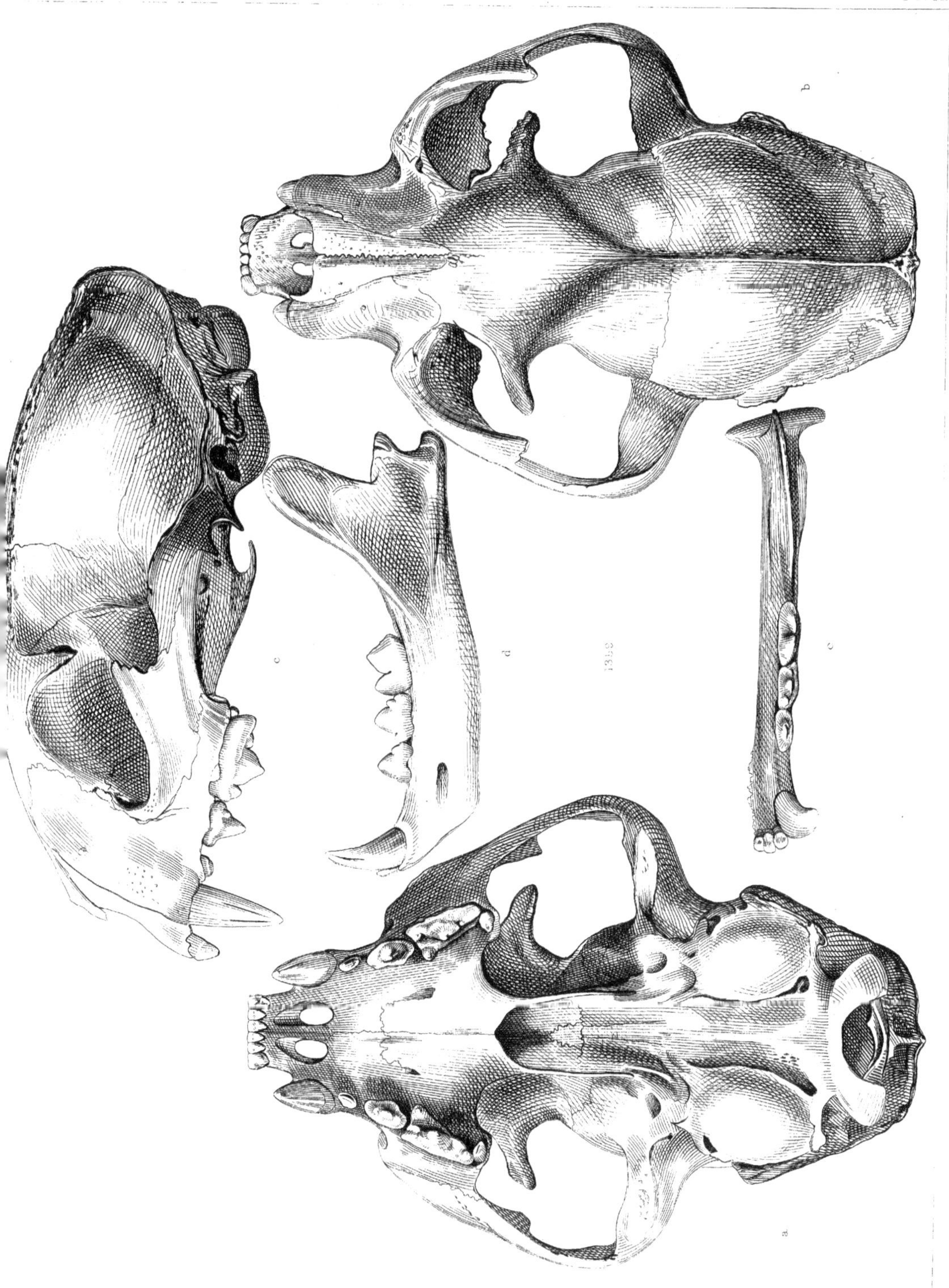

zeroth del. Dougal sc.

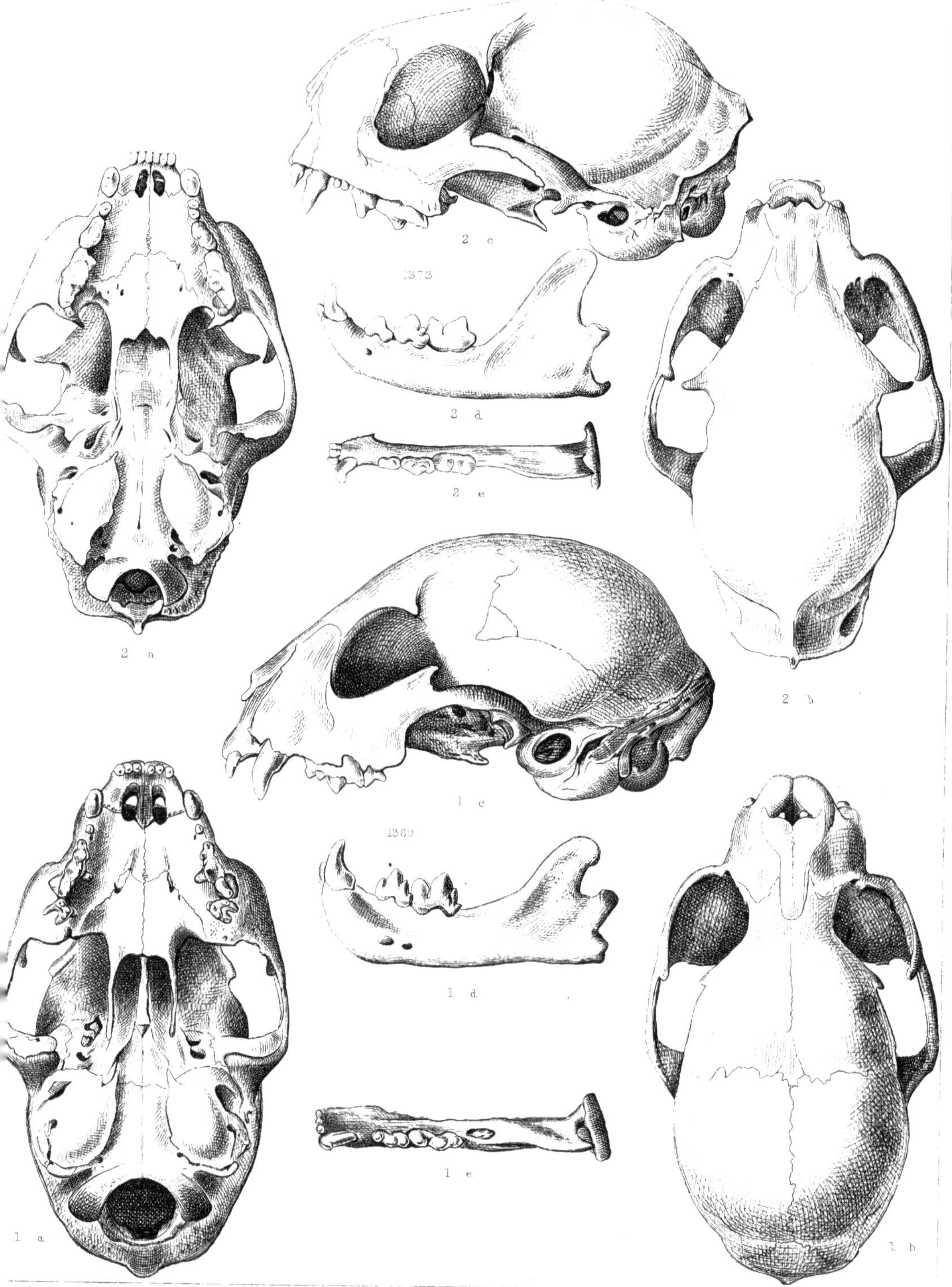

d. & Metzeroth del.

Dougal sc.

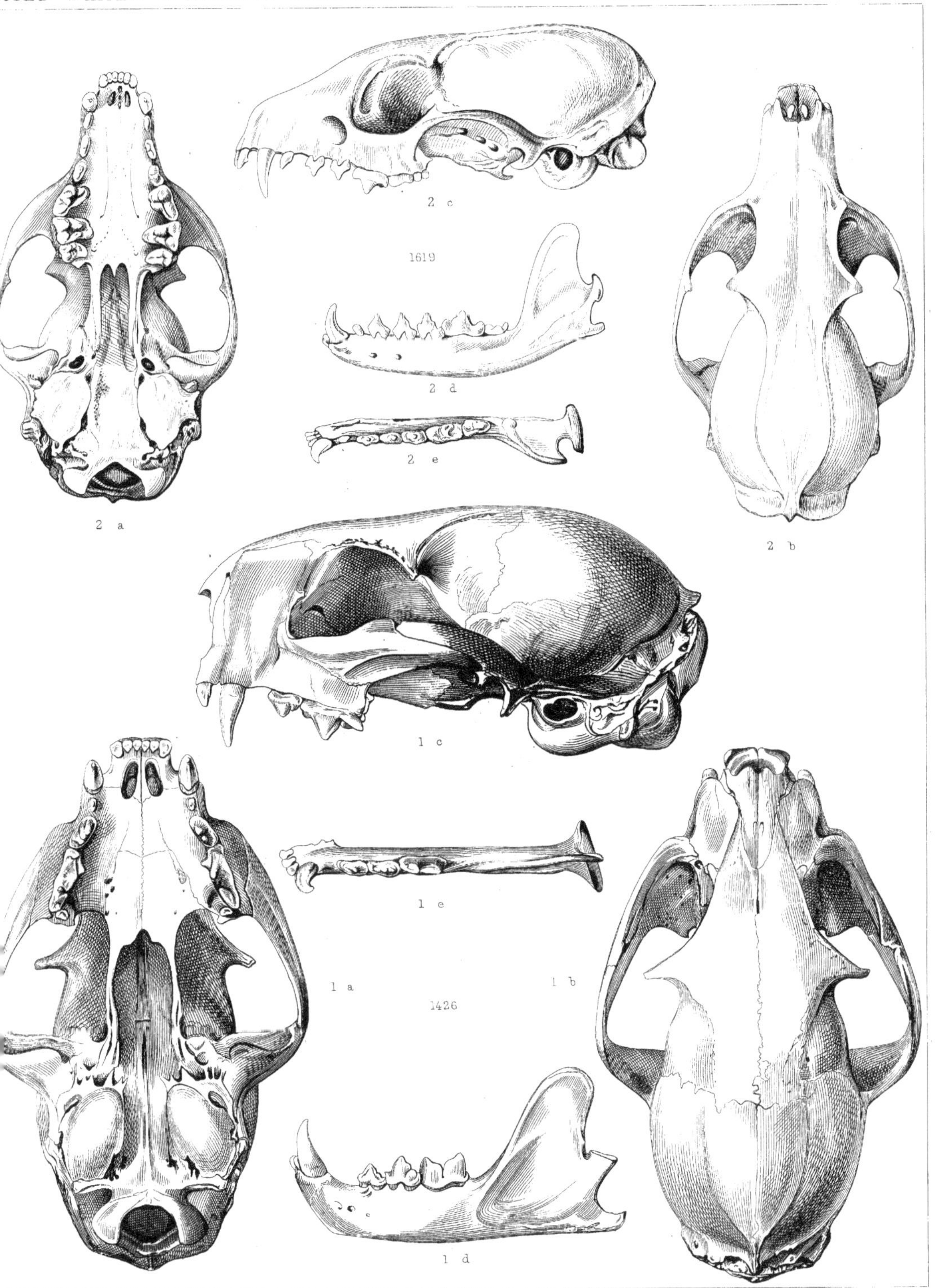

tzeroth del. Dougal sc.

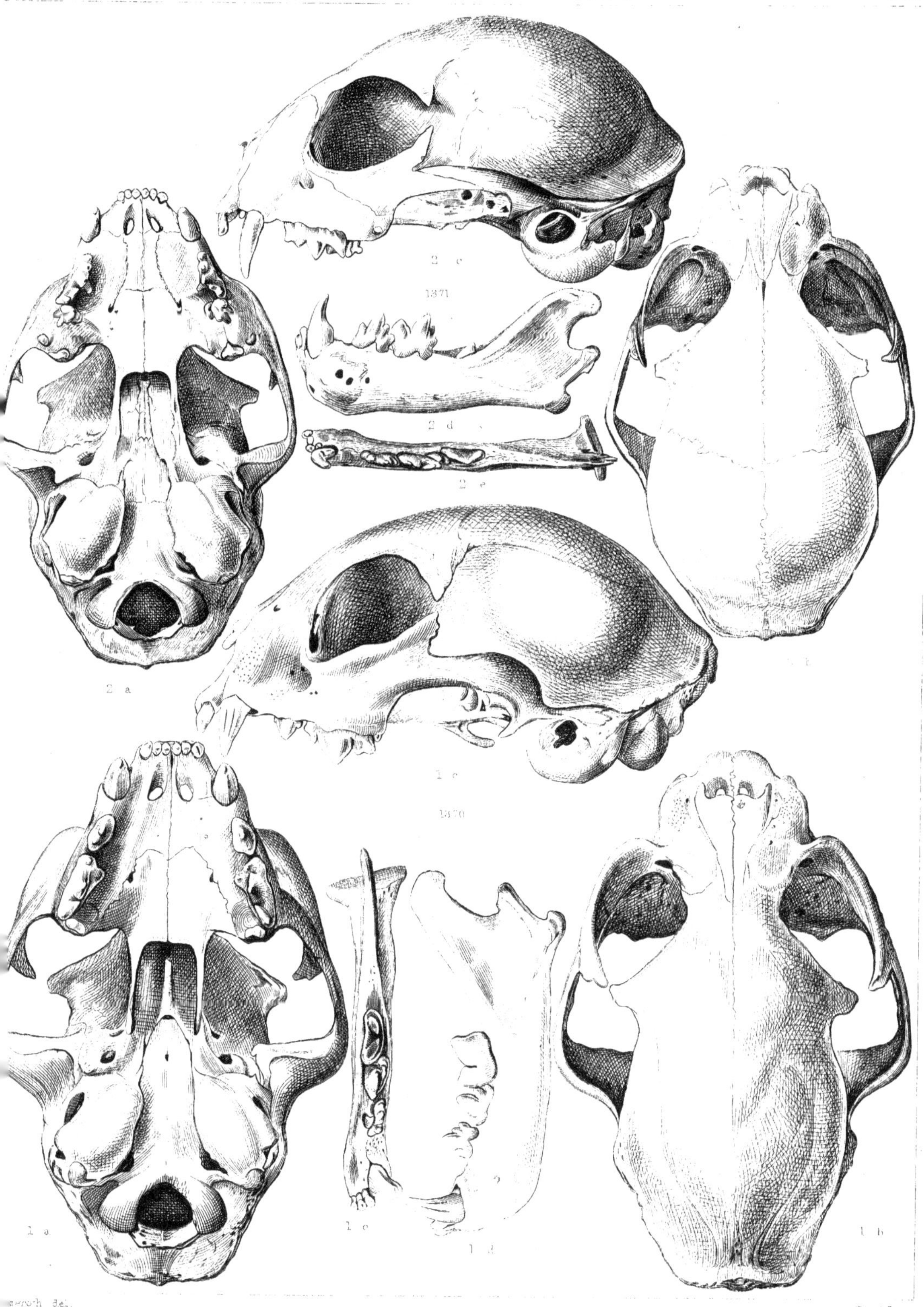

Dougal sc.

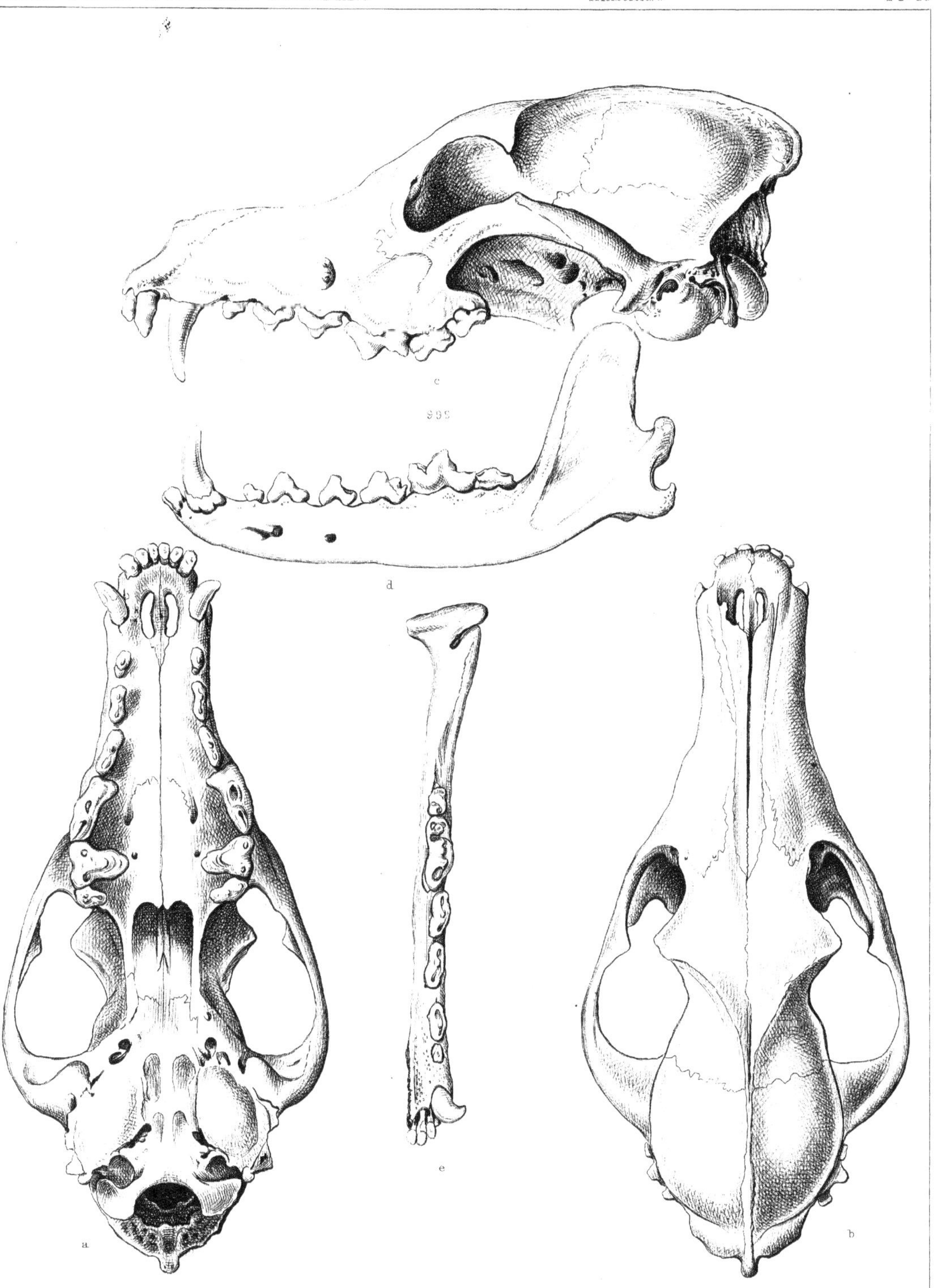

ichard. del. Dougal sc.

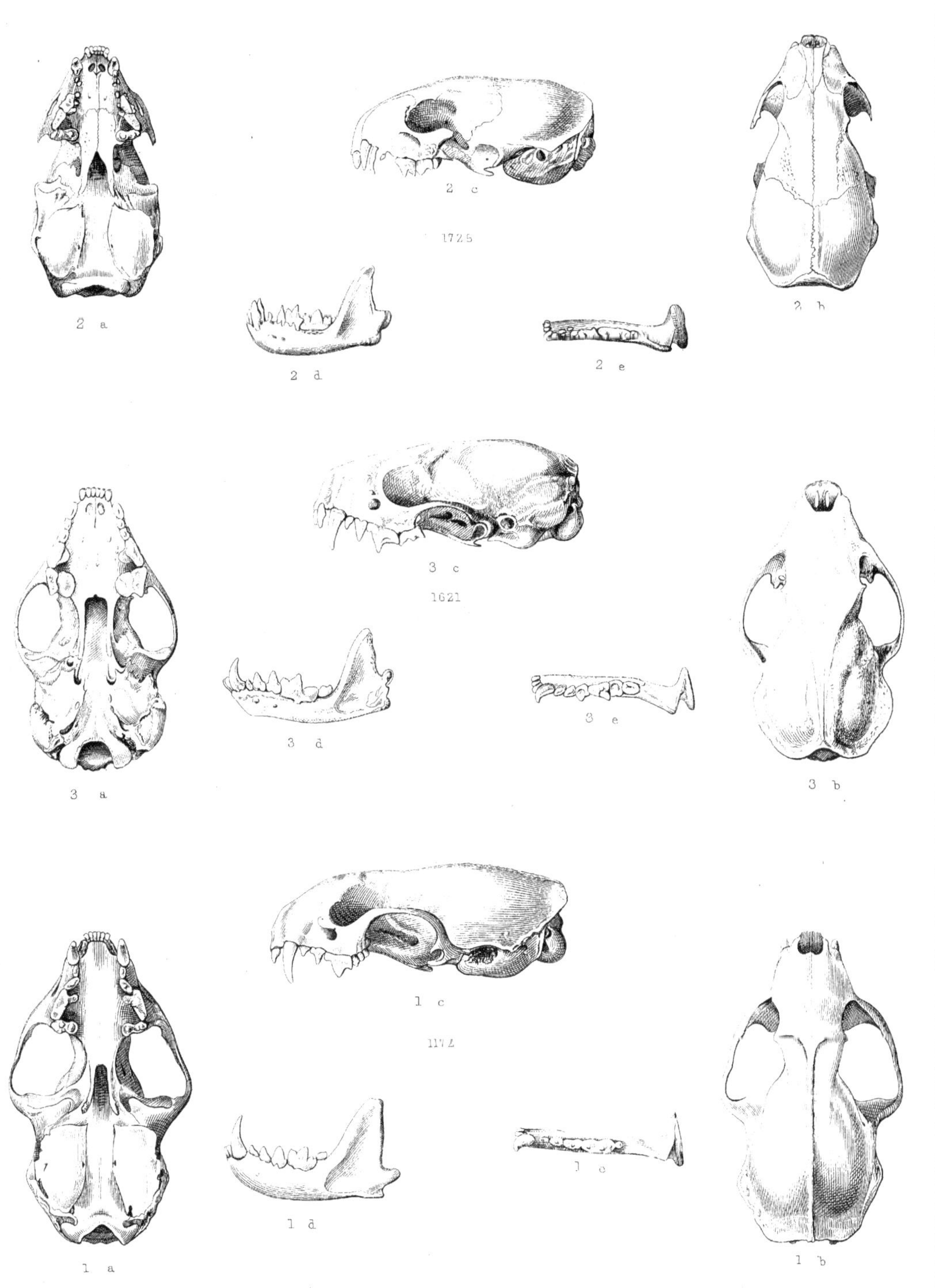

Weizeroth del. Dougal sc.

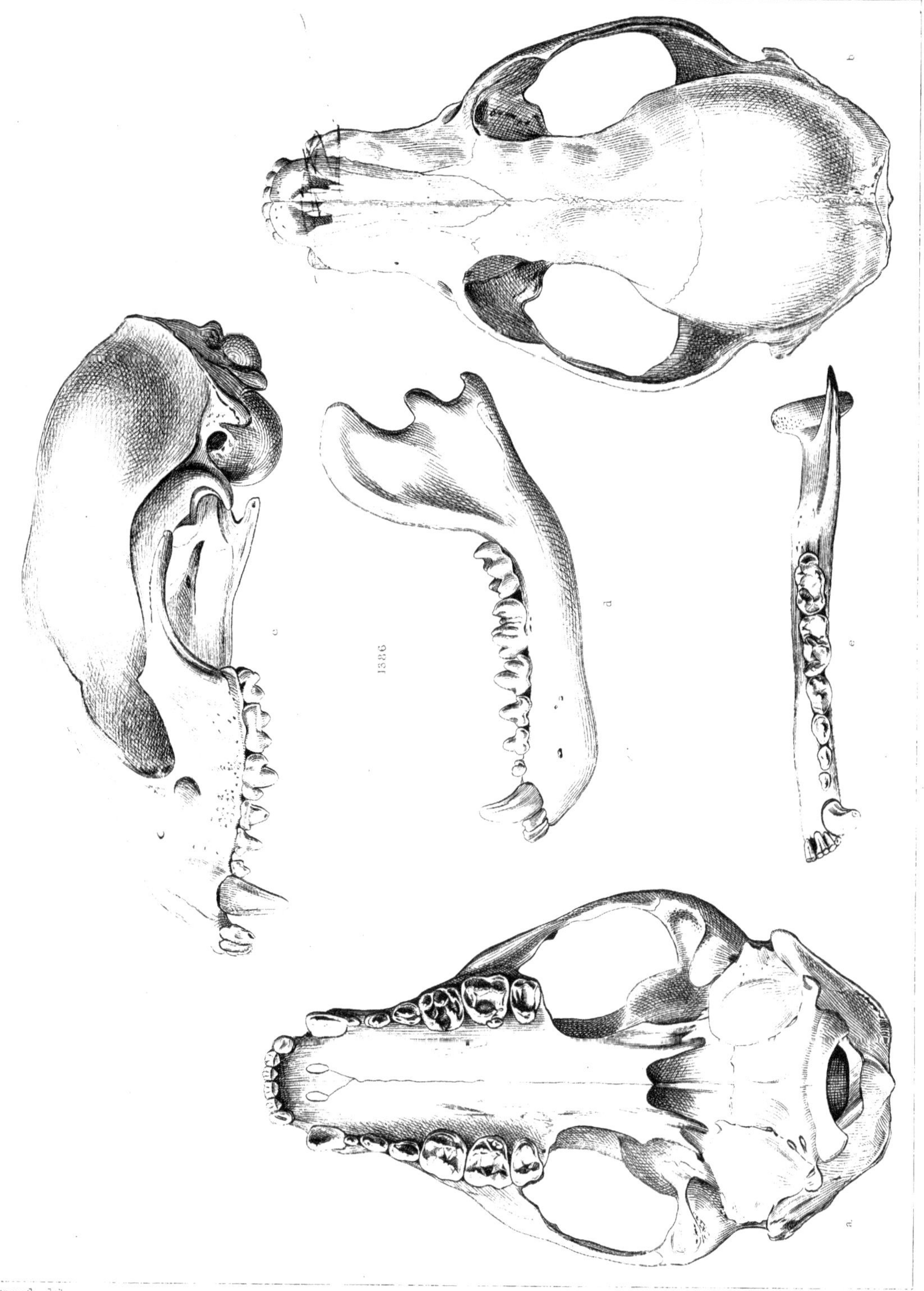

Staeroth del. Dougal sc.

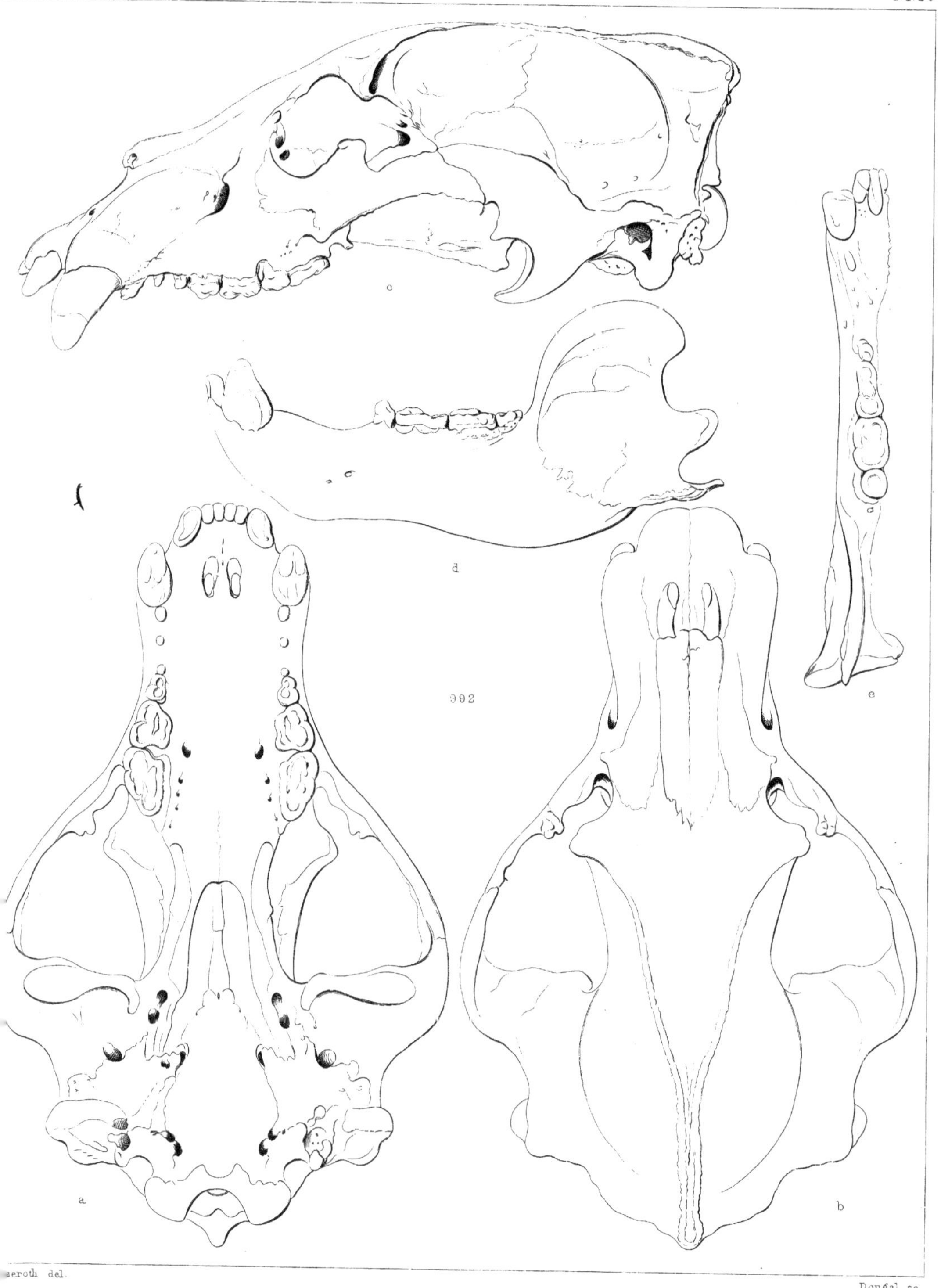

seroth del. Dougal sc.

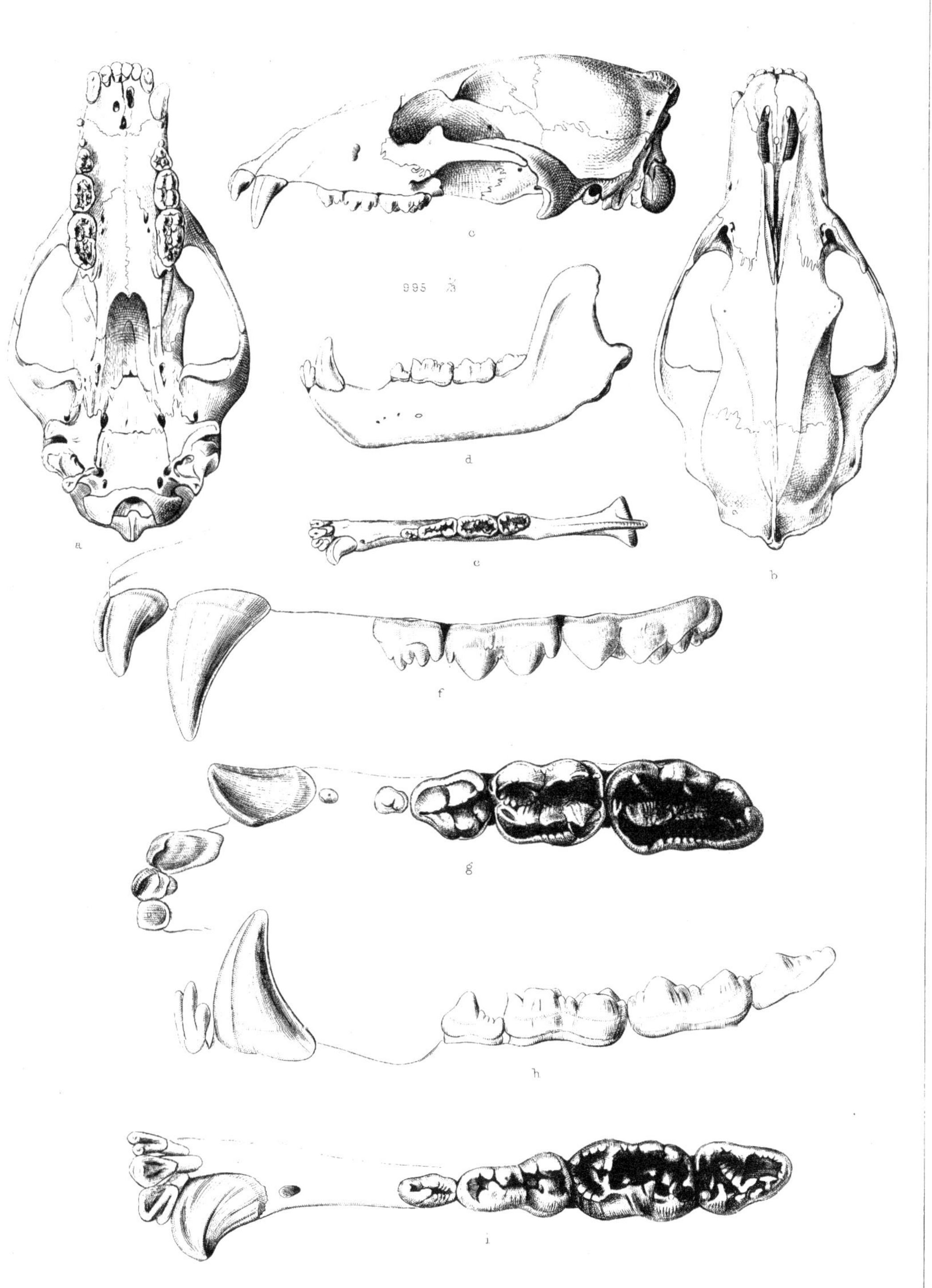

zeroth del. Dougal sc.

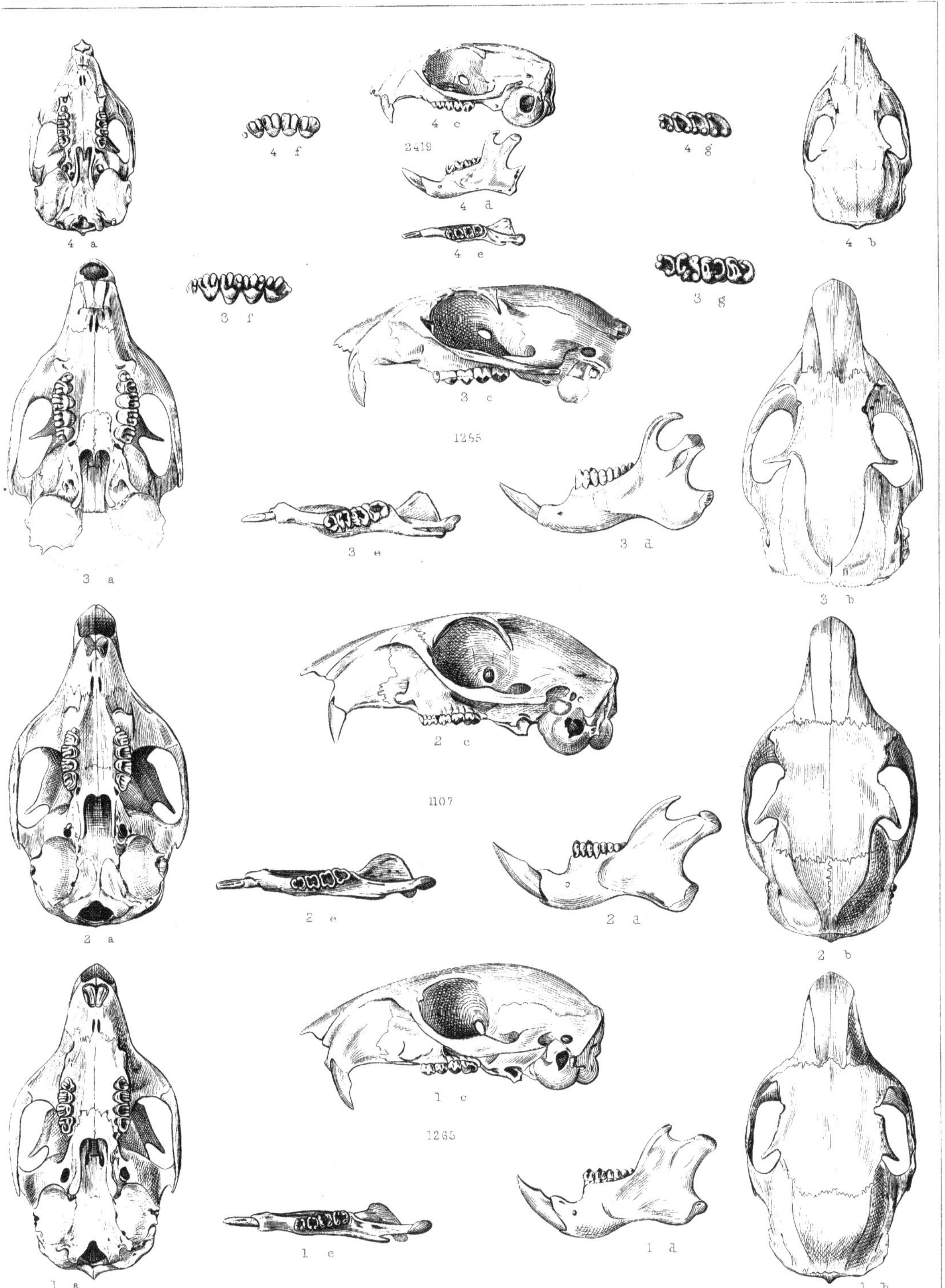

etzeroth del. Dougal sc.

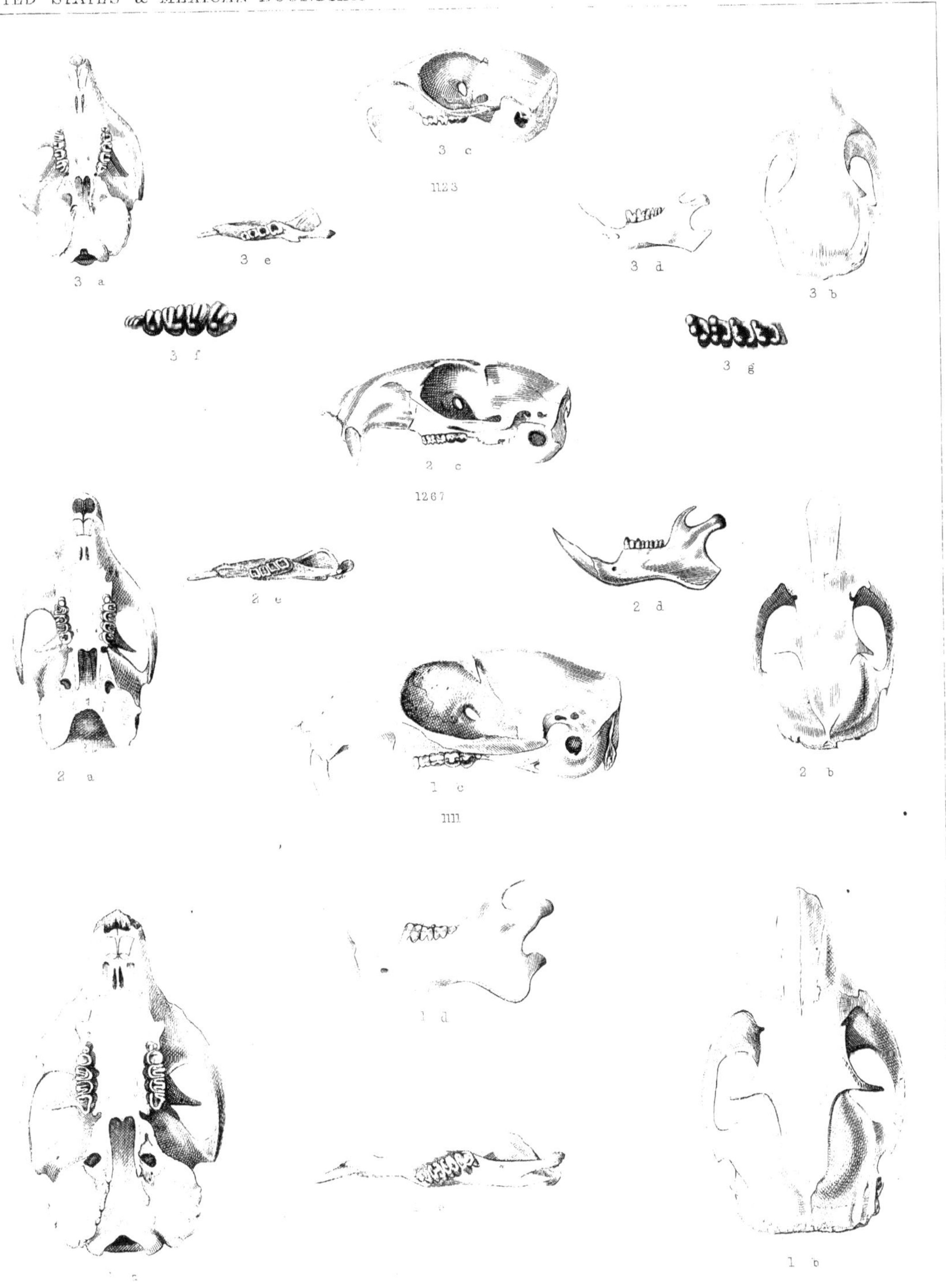

Mcxeroch del. Dougal sc.

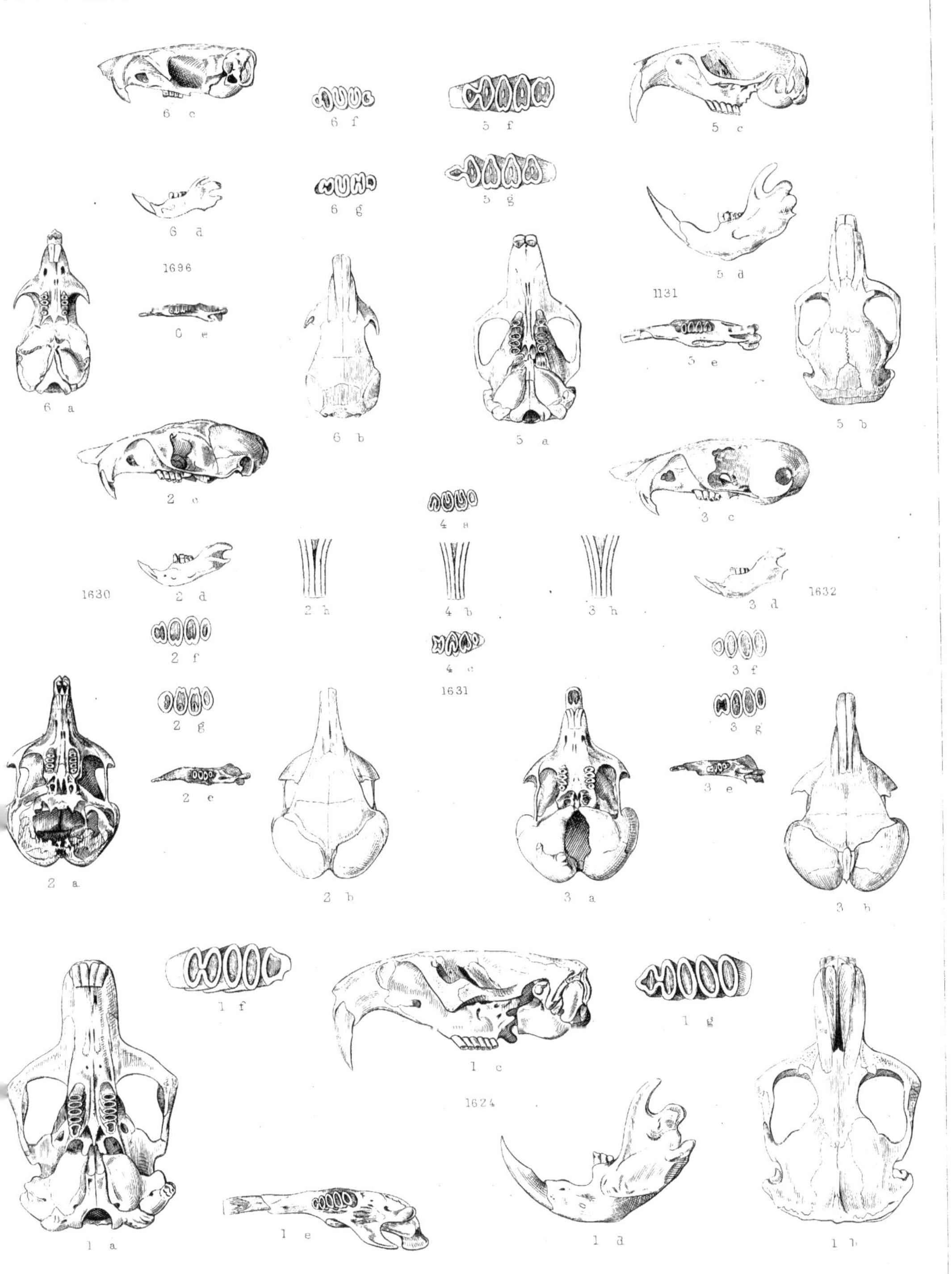

ard & Metzeroth del. Dougal sc.

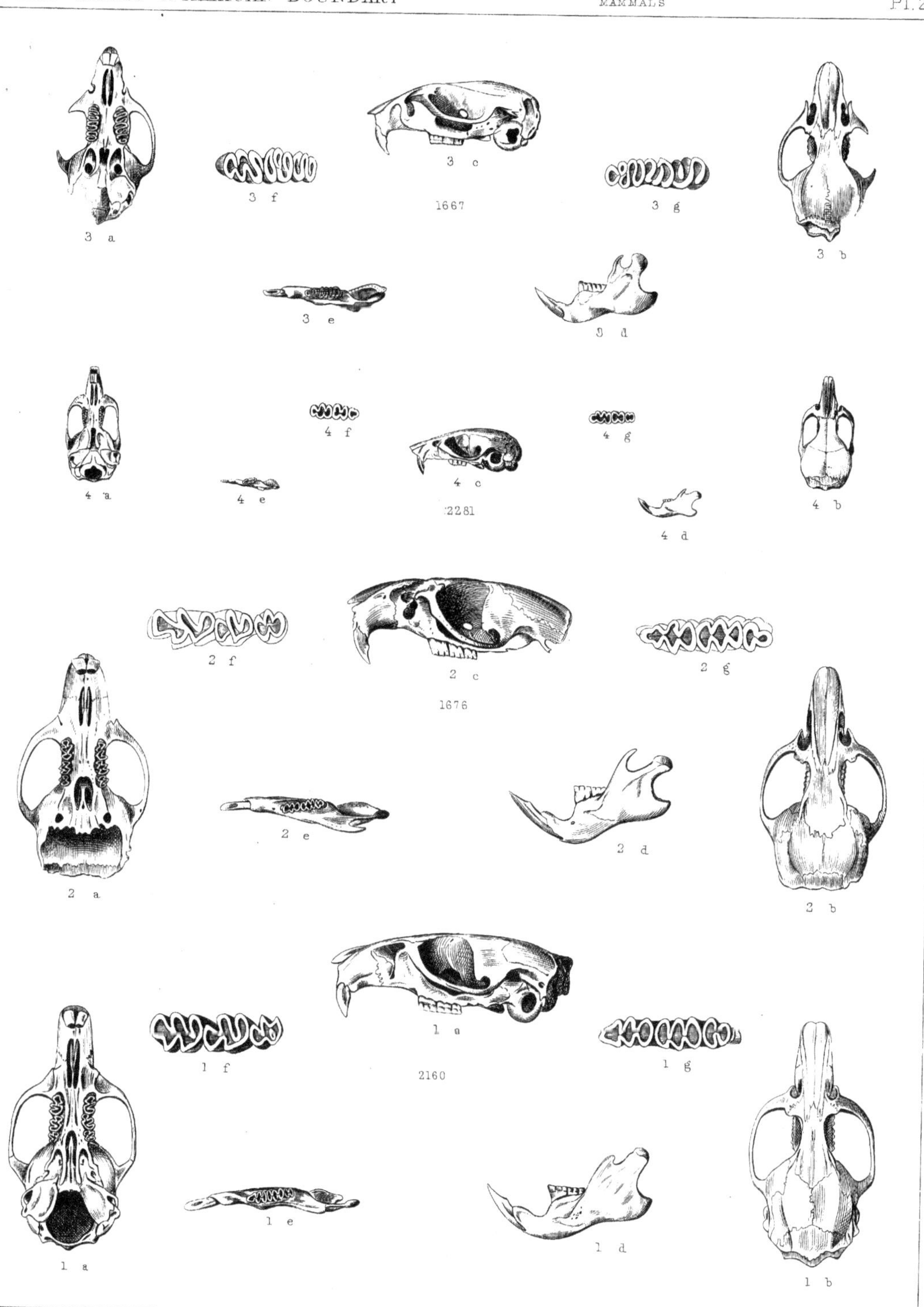

ichard del.

Dougal sc.

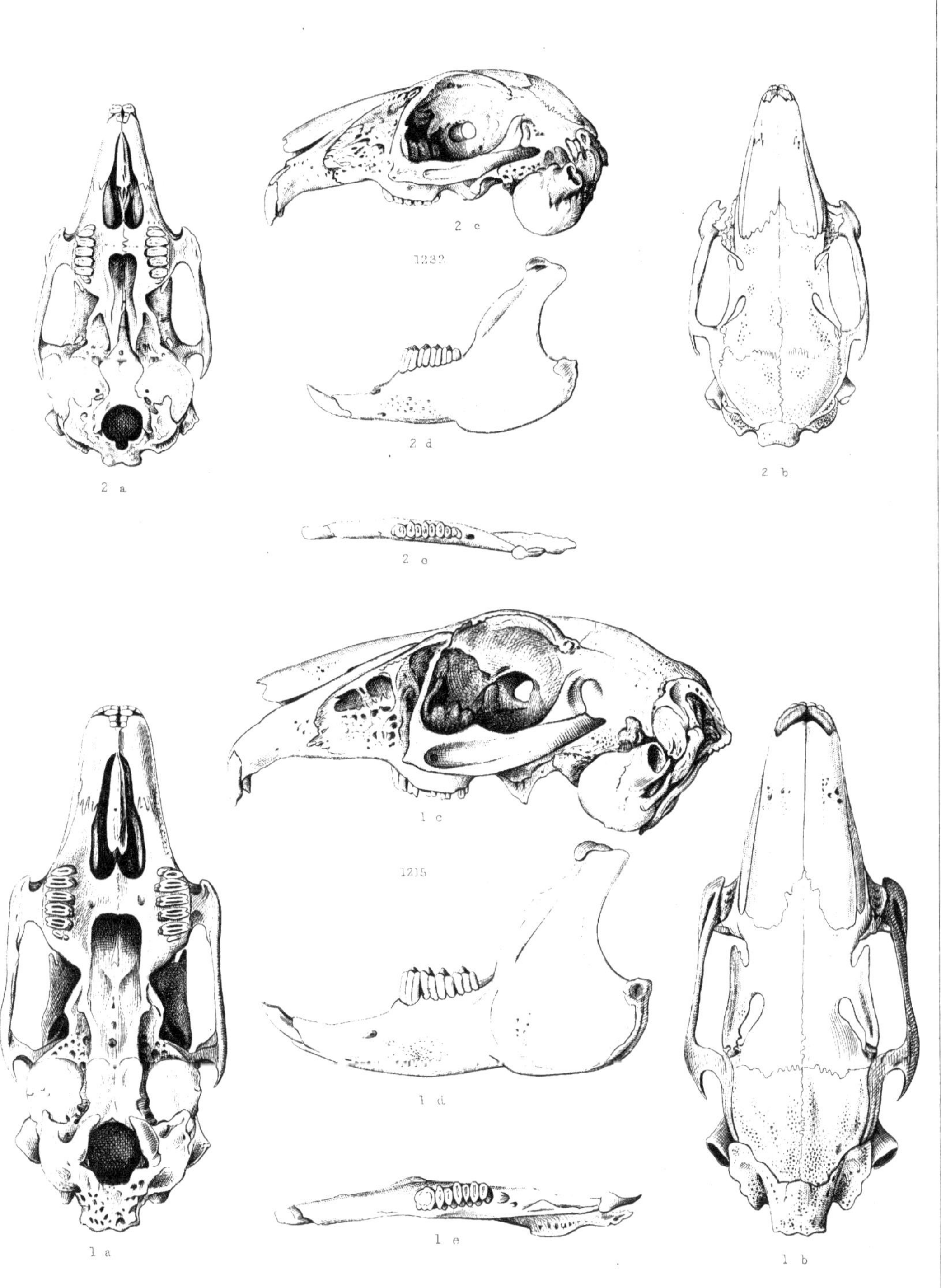

etzeroth del. Dougal sc.

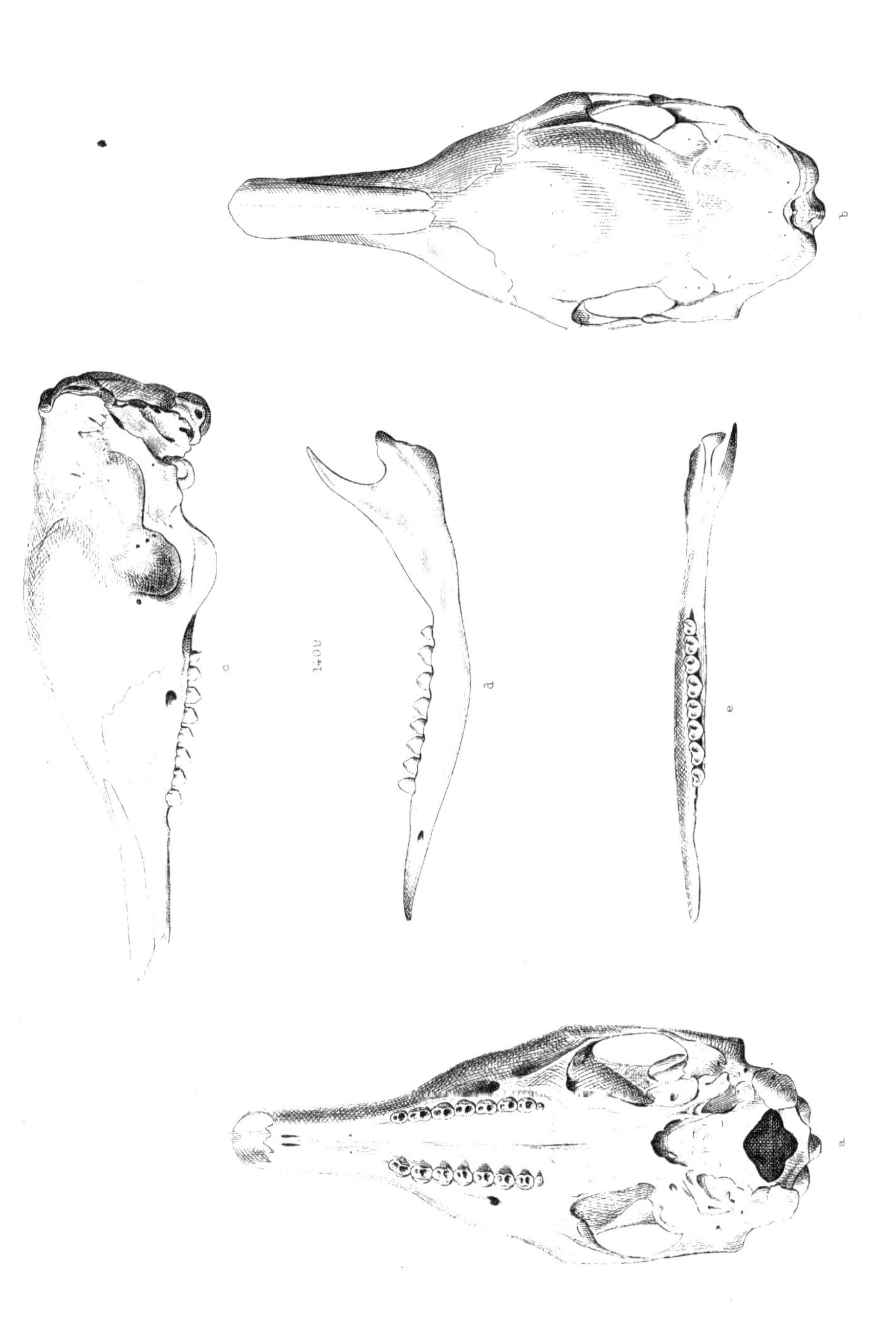
a
b
c
d
e
1409

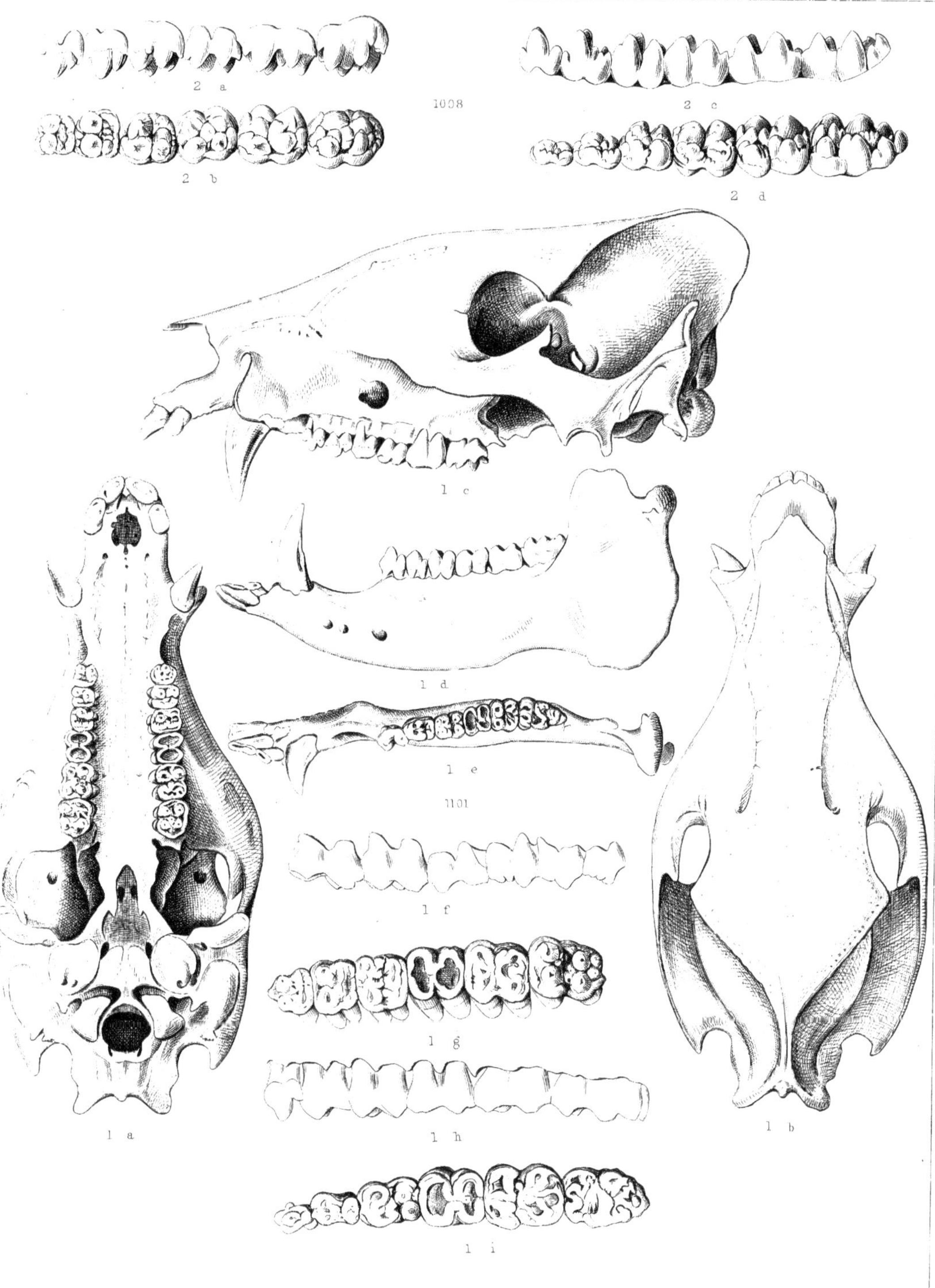
2 a
1008
2 c
2 b
2 d
1 c
1 d
1 e
1101
1 f
1 g
1 a
1 h
1 b
1 i

www.ingramcontent.com/pod-product-compliance
Lightning Source LLC
LaVergne TN
LVHW021425110826
845150LV00007B/2092